Ted the Shed

Adventures on my elderly Dad's allotment

by

Mandy Sutter

Illustrated by Janis Goodman

ISBN: 978-1-7385288-0-6

Cover image: Janis Goodman (front); Mandy Sutter (back)

Cover design: Mike Farren

Typesetting: Mike Farren

Acknowledgements

Enormous thanks to everyone who read and commented on this story, first when it was a blog and second when it was being turned into a book; to Janis for the wonderful drawings that hit just the right note; to Mike for making it into a book; and to Mr MS, who didn't mind me writing about him. Last but not least, thanks to Dad, who was always so proud every time I got something published.

For Ted

1923-2019

Part I – The first year

Late April 2010. Quids in

It all begins the day Dad rings me on the landline with shocking news. He is the only person we know who still uses a landline – so we keep it, despite the expense.

'We've been offered an allotment!' he shouts, without saying hello.

I understand his surprise. He put his name on the Parish Council's waiting list on his 80th birthday nearly seven years ago; had probably forgotten all about it. It was just after he and Mum moved north to be near me.

'What do you mean, we?' I say, glancing out of the kitchen window at the tiny back yard of the house I share with Mr Mandy Sutter. It is spring and dandelions have come up in all my plant pots. That is the level of gardening I am comfortable with.

He ignores my question. 'There's only one snag,' he says. 'It hasn't been cultivated for ten years or more. It's very overgrown.'

'That does sound like a snag,' I say, aiming for gentle discouragement. Never mind the fact that he is now prone to 'funny turns', has a bad toe that makes it difficult to walk and has never had an allotment before, just a vegetable patch in his Cotswolds garden that brought him nothing but misery.

But the fervour of a possible new venture is on him. Dad loves nothing more than a project. 'We'll go take a look at it, shall we?'

The plot is in a newly reclaimed area next to a well-established allotment community on the edge of our small town. It has been funded by Lottery money to try and reduce the 180-strong waiting list, Dad tells me as we walk and stumble the maze of narrow, uneven paths, passing impressive examples of recycling: ancient ceramic baths planted with potatoes, a greenhouse made entirely of windows, a shed made entirely of doors ('How do you know which one to open to go in?' asks Dad), rotting planks standing, leaning and lying for no apparent reason at all. There are animals. Chickens cluck, geese squawk and goats stand silently chewing.

We reach our potential plot. I stare at a chest high thicket of nettles, two quite sizeable trees and something I will later find described on the Royal Horticultural Society's website as 'a major weed problem' – Himalayan Balsam. I am mildly horrified. Faced with the reality, Dad will decide to turn the offer down. Surely. He stands, teetering slightly.

'Looks like a lot of hard work,' I say.

He grins. 'That's the beauty of it.'

'What?'

'It's in such a state they're letting us have it free for the first year. It's a beautiful spot, isn't it? The river is just on the other side of that fence! And is that a blackcurrant bush in the middle?' I peer but see only the powdery green hue of flowering nettles. Dad, taken out of school at 14 and set to work because his own father had lost his job, is thrifty to a fault and I am sure his appreciation of beauty is less to do with the river and more to do with the fact it isn't going to cost him a penny. And there's that word 'us' again. He goes on, 'Even if all we ever do is pick blackcurrants, we'll still be quids in!'

Now is the time to make my position clear. I have neither the time nor the inclination to take on a project like this. The only vegetables I recognise in growing form are potatoes and peas. Mr Mandy Sutter has zero interest in becoming a man of the soil so we can't count on him for help.

But somehow these words, though perfectly formed in my mind, don't come out of my mouth. The thing is, I haven't seen Dad so enthusiastic about anything for ages.

Soon after making their new start up north, Mum, disorientated in the unfamiliar flat, had a bad fall. She was never the same and died two years later. It was a terrible blow for Dad and me (I have no siblings). But today, Dad looks almost happy.

As for me, a heady, reckless feeling is on me, a known accompaniment to any doomed new project. I'm in my fifties now and the last time Dad and I

4

did anything horticultural together was at five when I made him 'garden salads' from grass, leaves and flowers, insisting that he ate them and watching to make sure he swallowed. Is it time this relationship moved on?

I find myself turning to him and smiling. 'It IS a beautiful spot.'

Early May 2010. Home-made tools

A week later, the Council say we're welcome to start work on our new plot. The first job is to see if there's anything of value on it, horticulturally speaking. I slash through the nettle jungle with a scythe, a vicious looking thing from the local tool shop. My hands tingle and throb despite my new gardening gauntlets – even my stings have stings.

Dad and Mr Mandy Sutter look on. They seem to be discussing the price of the scythe. 'Ten quid for that?' says Dad. 'I wouldn't give you ninety-nine pence for it.' He tells Mr MS that yesterday he made his own rake by hammering some spare 4″ nails into a piece of wood and attaching it to an old broom handle. Mr MS is clearly awestruck by the idea of anyone having spare 4″ nails lying around, let alone doing anything with them.

But Dad, brilliant with his hands, lives for making things. Soon after I was born, he took a Physics degree as a mature student and went on to become a geophysicist, troubleshooting on oil rigs all over the world. Fired up by figuring out better ways of doing things, he invented (and patented) several devices for the company he worked for.

In early retirement, he and Mum bought a Cotswolds house with a tumbledown cottage in the garden and he restored it single-handedly, learning each skill – bricklaying, plastering – as he went. In old age, although his projects have been smaller scale, they have been impressive in their own way. A few months ago, he made a reading lamp out of a baked bean tin and most recently when a front incisor fell out decided not to consult the dentist, but the local stationer. He bought an eraser and with his scalpel cut a rubber tooth to slot between his remaining ones. He soaked it in tea and red wine for a week to get the colour right.

© JANIS GOODMAN 2020

When family friends came to tea recently, his main preoccupation was to stop it falling out. He could only pretend to eat his biscuit and drink his tea. 'I think I got away with that,' he said, almost before they were out of the door, his triumph about his invention trumping everything in a way I found at once charming and chilling.

Back at the allotment, I go on hacking while Dad and Mr MS survey the two trees. They are at the back of the plot, near the fence. 'I could get those down in ten minutes if I could get hold of a good bow saw,' says Dad.

But all talk of tools is suddenly abandoned. All talk of past glories and future triumphs is put aside as the last sentinel ring of nettles falls and a fragrant-leaved centre of fruit bushes is revealed: gooseberries and blackcurrants (which we recognise and love) and redcurrants (which we identify later and could surely come to love if only we could find out what to do with them).

The berries are still green but their tight forms show among the leaves like pirate treasure. Later a knowledgeable friend/adversary will tell me that the bushes are so old and the berry-to-bush ratio so pitifully small that I should dig them out. But for the moment we all just turn to each other and grin. 'Wow!' says Mr MS.

'Blackcurrant jam!' I coo. 'Stewed fruit,' replies Dad. 'There's nothing like it, with a dollop of Cornish ice cream on top. Nice and soft.' Mr MS slides me a look. I know he's thinking that stewed blackcurrants and ice cream might be the one thing Dad can eat with his rubber tooth.

Mid-May 2010. Do Not Cut Down This Tree

'Hello, love,' says Dad on the phone on random occasions. 'I'm just setting off for the plot.'

Dad's style of communication, while very direct on some matters, is indirect on others. The above declaration is his way of asking me to join him. It's lovely to be asked of course, even indirectly. But it's so long since Dad last had a job that he forgets other people still have to work for a living. Even with a half-baked job like freelance writing, I can't always drop everything to join him.

I try turning the tables and inviting him. But this doesn't work, perhaps because a) he likes to be the inviter not the invitee and b) he has reached an age where one event per day is enough.

'Oh no, love,' he'll say. 'I'm thinking of going to Tesco's that day.'

The upshot is that for the next two or three weeks we don't manage to visit the plot at the same time. This isn't my vision of a shared endeavour. I work mainly on clearing and weeding the central area where the fruit bushes are. I can't always tell what Dad has been doing and he tends not to let on, even when asked. I remember his dislike of being questioned.

Then work takes me away for a few nights. When I leave, there are two trees on the allotment. When I come back, there are one and a half. I shouldn't really be surprised. In the gaps in every conversation since he got the plot (and even when there haven't been gaps) Dad has been saying, 'That ash has got to come down. Don't you think?'

Mr MS tells me the full story. Dad, after a brief consultation with the Parish Councillor in charge of allotments, felled the tree with a small handsaw then cut it into short lengths unaided.

'Don't look at me like that!' he adds. 'I offered to help. But he pretended he couldn't hear.'

It's true that Dad's hearing aid – bending his ears forward with his cupped hands – doesn't always work.

'I was worried he'd have one of his turns,' Mr MS goes on. 'His face got redder and redder!'

Having witnessed Dad's phenomenal work ethic my entire life, I can imagine this only too well. When I fell single thirty years ago and had to move house, he insisted on installing my new kitchen (not the distressed pine one I liked, but the oak one he said was better wood) in one weekend. He worked grim-faced while Mum and I stood by anxiously, unable to help but unable to go and do anything else either. 'Oh dear,' my Mum said when they left. 'And it was meant to be a NICE weekend.'

Now that he's in his late eighties, there's an added stressor – he has started saying things like, 'this will probably kill me.' It makes for a nerve-wracking watch. The intimation of frailty that would make some people take it easy only serves to goad him into ever more extreme acts of DIY.

I feel sorry for Mr MS. 'Never mind,' I say. 'Now why don't you pop to the kitchen and make me a nice cup of tea?'

He trundles off, calmer already.

And there's more. At the allotment a few days later, I'm shocked to see a cardboard sign on the tree that is still standing. 'DO NOT CUT DOWN THIS TREE!' it says. In smaller writing it says 'The Other Tree Should Not Have Been Cut Down Either!'

I'm both offended and mortified. That exclamation mark! Those capital letters! But looking at it again, the cut tree does look awful. Dad has lopped it off at chest height, making it look somehow more cut-down than if he'd taken it off at the root. It looks like an unpardonable allotment crime.

The sign on the tree reads:

DO NOT CUT DOWN THIS TREE!

THE OTHER TREE SHOULD NOT HAVE BEEN CUT DOWN EITHER

© JAN IS GOODMAN 2020

I stare at the notice some more. Who has put it there? The writing's neat and it has been dated, which speaks of officialdom. But it's unsigned, and the anonymity is unsettling. Perhaps one of our allotment neighbours has written it. Or perhaps a group of them!

I walk home slowly, the gardening idyll souring with every step. I imagine a future of frosty looks, trashed cabbages, a dead rabbit hung from the (remaining) tree, allotment vigilantes armed with hoes standing over us until we pack up our bargain B&Q fork and trowel set and go.

Mr MS is in his favourite arm chair, reading the paper. 'Who wrote the notice? I beg him. 'Who, who, who?'

'I dunno,' he says, turning the pages. 'What's for tea?'

But it's alright. The sign turns out to be from the Council and the next morning Dad gets a letter saying so. The letter is much more polite than the sign, focussing on the importance of conservation. Dad writes an equally civil letter back explaining that he is 'very deaf' and must have misheard the Councillor when he said the trees should stay.

11

I am profoundly relieved. I can go back to smiling and saying good morning to everyone at the allotments without fear of turned backs or dark mutterings. And our plot looks better with just the one tree. We have shade but we also have sun.

I consider moving the Council's sign to the stump of the cut down tree, a joke I think Dad will appreciate. Unexpectedly, he vetoes it. 'We don't want to get anyone's back up, do we?' he says.

Mid-May 2010. Views to die for

You may be wondering what possessed an elderly man to leave the comfort, civilisation and creamy stonework of his birthplace in the Cotswolds and move to Yorkshire, land of millstone grit and gale force winds. The answer is my mother. Dad, like many men of his generation, had an 'anything for an easy life' philosophy. A few months after I'd met Mr MS and moved him into my house to make an honest man out of him, Mum decided she'd like to live near us and Dad, despite reservations, went along with it. Mum and Dad were installed up here within the year, in a flat with amazing views on the posh side of town.

I was a little worried. I felt pressured to make my new relationship with Mr MS work and thought Mum and Dad had underestimated the loneliness of living with no friends nearby. On the plus side we could see each other easily and regularly, without the pressure of having to stay in each other's houses for an entire weekend.

Dad, always a loner, didn't seem to need any friends. It was different for Mum. Unfamiliar with the layout of their new flat she got up to go for a pee one night and came a cropper in the bathroom. Following that, with the flat a mile out of town and up a steep hill, she couldn't get out and about independently. She began to feel lonely and to look forward to a time when she'd be admitted to a care home and have 'people to talk to.' She bought a set of nylon nighties in anticipation. 'They'll be easy to wash and dry when I widdle myself,' she said.

She lived for another two years then was taken by a stroke. Dad blamed the move North. Old school in his thinking about children and parents, he didn't understand my grief. 'But you left home years ago!' he kept saying. He also wouldn't tolerate my maternal clucking around him. 'I don't need you to pop round here every five minutes. I've got to sit here on my own until I get used to it.'

As an only child I had often felt outnumbered by my parents, but now Mum was gone and it was Dad who was outnumbered by Mr MS and me. We did our best not to gang up on him but sometimes he felt it anyway, accusing us of being 'against' him.

He mentioned suicide. I worried, but my GP told me not to fret unless Dad's proposed methodology became detailed and included timings. 'Please just get a gun and shoot me' was apparently nothing to worry about. Besides, elderly people had a dozen different ways to end their lives, the GP added, from leaving rumpled rugs at the top of stairs, to climbing stepladders in ill-fitting slippers. I didn't know how to take this. Was it supposed to comfort me? The funny thing was that it did while at the same time scaring the hell out of me.

I wished, not for the first time, that I had children of my own to focus on. It would have helped Dad too, I think. Mr MS's children would have done at a pinch, but he had none either. At least we had Dog MS though, beloved by all.

Mr MS's and my fledgling union did its best to blossom in these circumstances. Against a backdrop of grief, love, difficulty, misunderstanding and thwarted longing stood the advent of the allotment. No wonder Dad grabbed the opportunity with both hands, plus all the forks, spades, trowels and mysterious little pointy tools he could muster. No wonder I grabbed it too.

Late May 2010. Raised on bricks or blocks

'We need somewhere to keep our tools,' Dad announces one morning on the phone. 'Stop 'em getting pinched. Somewhere for when it rains, so we can sit and watch all the other buggers get soaked.'

His robust view of things startles me but a quick internet search reveals a shed for sale at B&Q for just £100. I ring Dad back. But suddenly he is cool. 'Let's play it by ear. There's no hurry.'

I'm surprised then when he rings the next morning to tell me he spent yesterday afternoon driving around DIY warehouses and ended up ordering the B&Q shed. He likes going out in his tiny new red Peugeot. Ditching his old car was a wrench because he and Mum had driven 'as far as the moon' together in it. But a £2K scrappage allowance swung it. When he talks about his new car, as he often does, he says, 'it's a pretty flimsy affair. But what do you expect when you buy a vehicle for £5K? And I must say at 87 I never thought I'd be driving a car said to have 'cheeky looks'.'

CHEEKY LOOKS

Ready-made items rarely satisfy Dad: he usually modifies the things he buys. Cheeky Looks is no exception. He has jacked the driving seat up with a plank of wood, wired in an extra loudspeaker and let half the air out of the tyres to create a 'softer ride.'

But back to the shed, which I imagine will also be subject to modifications. It's arriving at his flat tomorrow. 'The only problem is how we get it to the allotment,' he says. 'Some of the pieces are pretty big. But they'd probably fit on your roof rack. I reckon we can manage it between the three of us. What do you think?'

What I think is that our plot is a very long way from the road where we can park the car. But guessing that Dad won't accept this objection (or indeed any objection) I say nowt and hatch a plan to hire a man and a van, perhaps without telling anyone. Before I can put this into action, Mr Mandy Sutter takes charge. He arranges for a local removal firm to shift the shed, giving Dad time to carry out a few reinforcements first.

'Did he agree to that?' I ask Mr MS.

'Of course,' says Mr MS. 'He also said the shed was a pretty flimsy affair, but what else could you expect when you bought a shed for £100?'

Council rules and regs state that 'huts' on the new plots 'shall be constructed of timber' and 'shall stand no bigger than 4' x 6'.' This rule will soon be flouted by an allotment neighbour's gargantuan polytunnel. 'I didn't realise it was going to be that big,' he will say sheepishly. And in the old part of the allotments, huts are made out of all sorts and the goat allotment shed is the size of a detached bungalow. But I'm relieved there's an official limit.

The regs also say huts must be 'raised on bricks or blocks.' Apparently, the allotments are prone to flooding. Some plot holders have ignored this stipulation and raised their sheds on nothing but half inch paving stones, though our neighbour has raised hers on two-foot stilts. It looks like a tree house, with no tree.

On the day, the removal men manhandle the bits of shed down to the allotment and I follow with flask and flapjacks. I see that Dad has built a solid wooden base about a foot high.

The guys leave and Dad proceeds to put the shed up single-handedly. It takes hours but he just won't allow us to help much, no matter how anxiously we buzz around trying to. I think about Mum. It is the 'new kitchen' scenario all over again. Mr MS has to content himself with erecting a self-assembly bench.

But the result is a smashing little shed in the dappled shade of the wych elm. Dad finally accepts a coffee and a sit down, though he refuses a snack. Mr MS, traumatised by watching an 87 year old man put up a shed on his own, wolfs flapjacks silently. As for me, I hope it rains soon so we can sit inside and watch all the other buggers get soaked.

Early June 2010. Ted the Shed

The shed awakens something profound in Dad.

'A chap could live in a hut like this,' he says, one sunny morning when we manage to visit the plot at the same time. He opens the shed door. 'In all this lovely peace and quiet.'

I dump my rucksack on the bench. Dad has tied twine to an eyelet on the door and winds the other end in a figure of eight around a coat hook he has fixed on the shed front. 'All you'd need is a camp bed to doss down on.'

'Wouldn't you miss your Sky TV?'

'Not really. I'd have all my tools around me. Could do something useful in the evenings instead of sitting around getting brain rot.'

I laugh, nervously. Much as I love the allotments, there's an edgy feel to them after dark. Having said that, one of the bigger sheds near the entrance has a chimney, and we often see smoke rise from it.

When Mum and Dad first moved up here, I told them the story of the eighteenth-century hermit associated with our town. He lived in a hut up on the moors with no running water and grew potatoes to feed himself. He was a well-known figure and they named a local pub after him.

Mum was horrified. 'And what about going to the toilet?' she asked. 'And washing?'

I couldn't have agreed more. But Dad was nonchalant about such niceties. 'That chap had the right idea,' he said.

'What about food?' I ask now.

'Oh, I don't need much these days,' says Dad. He gets his cut-off Tesco's orange juice bottle full of screws out of the shed and starts rummaging in it.

I sit on the bench, remembering a visit to Mum and Dad's Cotswolds home twenty-five years ago. I hadn't visited for a couple of months and in that time, Dad had been hard at work in the attic space. He invited me up for a look. I picked my way carefully up the very steep wooden steps and pulled myself up through the hatch.

'Wow!' was all I could say.

Under the sloping beams on one side, all Dad's tools hung over an old workbench. On the other side of the space stood an old toilet and a large fridge freezer.

'How did you get that those up here?' I asked.

'With difficulty,' said Dad, beaming.

He went over and opened the fridge door. Inside I saw six bottles of his homemade orange wine. He opened the freezer section to show three jumbo tubs of Cornish ice cream and two trays of ice cubes. 'What more could anyone want?' he said. 'Care for a tipple?' I usually avoided Dad's orange wine but, on this occasion, even knowing it would put me out of action for the rest of the day, I couldn't bring myself to refuse.

At lunch time, we went carefully back downstairs and into the kitchen where Mum was busy putting food onto plates. 'It's amazing what Dad's done up there in the attic, isn't it?' I said, or probably slurred. She pulled a face. 'I don't know about that,' she said. 'He can't hear me at all when he's up there. No matter how loud I shout.'

Poor Mum. Because she could be a nag, at the time I thought 'no wonder'. But now, in a long-term relationship myself, I have every sympathy.

Fast forward to the allotment again, where Dad has picked out four longish screws and laid them on the top step of the shed. He looks over. 'I'd have my air rifle, of course,' he says.

'Of course,' I say, wonderingly. It's so different now, I think. He lives alone, so there's no one to get away from any more and certainly no shortage of privacy. Yet he still contemplates shed life. His desire for self-sufficiency, for going back to basics, obviously runs deep. I can't help wishing Mum had known that all those years ago.

Mid-June 2010. Room to grow

When Dad first took possession of the allotment in April, it was too overgrown to plant anything. By the time letters about cutting down trees are sent and answered and the shed is up and customised with dozens of little shelves and tool racks, it is past peak planting time altogether. Neighbouring allotmenteers decided from the outset that it was too late and restricted themselves to clearance. Others went at it like crazy and planted their plots up with vegetable seedlings.

'That's not gardening,' says Dad. 'That's shopping.'

Our approach has ended up falling somewhere between, not that we've planned it. Some might say it's characterised by indecision and disorganisation. I prefer the word 'organic.'

It was obvious that we'd keep the blackcurrant bushes and some of the brambles because we like blackcurrants and blackberries. We've ended up keeping the redcurrant bushes too. They take up quite a lot of room. The shed is another winner in this respect, as is the tree, the tree stump and the bench. I'm planning a compost heap and a water butt and Mr MS thinks it's a good idea to leave a ring of weeds and grass around the bushes because it's a bit like a path.

But that still leaves a heck of a lot of space for growing things. Progress here is hampered by Dad's and my 'artistic differences.' We agreed from the get-go, or so I thought, that we'd restrict ourselves to clearing and weeding until we had a better idea of the space, then discuss what was still good for planting and where.

Or perhaps it was just me that agreed it, and only with myself. Dad slips down one evening with 30 seed potatoes and plants them any which way along the back fence, in the area I'd told him was ideally suited to taller plants like Jerusalem artichokes and sunflowers.

21

'I thought it would be good to get something in the ground,' he says by way of explanation. 'I mean, what have we got to lose?'

I fume, but only inwardly, because this is Dad I'm dealing with and although communication can be robust on his side, we have no history of it ever being so on mine. I have always tended to keep quiet and vote with my feet.

I decide that if that's how it's going to be then I'm going to plant some crops of my own. Over the next week, I dig a long bed at the side of the plot. This involves levelling a mound the size and shape of a human grave (unnerving) and pulling out miles of gnarled nettle root, like unravelling a vast underground yellow jumper. The afternoon the soil is finally clear, I realise I have to plant it up before Dad riddles it with more seed potatoes so I stay until after dark planting everlasting spinach and kale. They are in seedling form, whatever Dad may say about that. I lob in a few turnip seeds for good measure.

I ring Dad, tell him what I've done and express my hope that he'll share in the produce. But he says he doesn't care much for spinach. 'It all goes into a mulch doesn't it?' He dislikes kale too, saying 'you can't get it out of your mouth.' I don't even mention the turnips, as the seeds probably won't come up and even I consider them an acquired taste.

The next evening, he rings and says he has just come back from planting 40 seed potatoes. 'Home Guard,' he elaborates.

'What? Where?' I almost shout.

'Oh, in that big area near the front.'

At least he hasn't planted them in 'my' patch. But I know the spot he means. I had started to create a path there, to lead from the grass ring to a future gate. I bet he's gone right across it. 'Only a few seed potatoes left to go!' he says, triumphant.

I fume inwardly. 'How many?'

'Oh, twenty. Or thereabouts.'

What seemed like too much planting space suddenly seems too little. No matter how big the allotment seemed at first, I begin to question whether there is room on it for two people related to each other. I rant to Mr MS. 'It's chaos down there! And it's completely pointless, what he's done. It's too late to plant seed potatoes now.'

Mr MS looks up from his book. He has very little interest in potatoes, or in the right time for planting them. But he makes an effort. 'Oh well,' he says, in a kindly tone. 'He's always been a bit of an individualist. What did you expect?'

One of Mr MS's chief duties is to remind me what my Dad is like and to find it quaint that knowing this I allow myself to go on being irritated and infuriated by him. I decide to perform a classic relationship preservation technique; to go out of the room containing Mr MS and into another one.

Of course, it's true about Dad. He was never a team player. As a technical trouble-shooter on oil rigs, he led crews, but when facing a particularly difficult problem he would often work through the night 'when the other chaps were in bed' to ensure the job got done right. His thinking was more lucid alone. His shyness no doubt came into it too.

At Mum's funeral, I told Mr MS that I hoped to 'get to know Dad better' now he was on his own. Of course, that's exactly what's happening now, and it's not quite what I imagined. Sitting on the sofa working my way to the bottom of a tub of rum and raisin ice cream I admit to myself, more honestly, that I was hoping he might start to view me more as an adult, less of a child.

Mind you, given his opinion of most adults, that might not amount to much. You can count the people he respects on the fingers of one hand (not including the thumb.) Spooning down mouthfuls of cold sweetness, I realise that I'd also hoped, without any evidence, that he might adhere more to the softer, sociable side of his nature without the frequent ding-dongs he and Mum engaged in. It strikes me now that that was wishful thinking and that in fact, Mum probably had a civilising effect on him. Without her he's free to go his own sweet way and answer to nobody, especially not his daughter. Rum and raisin ice cream despatched, I sigh and turn on the TV for a rerun of Inspector Morse.

I'm struck anew by the awkward relationship between Morse and his subordinate Lewis. Practical, full of platitudes and playing it relentlessly by the book, Lewis continually annoys his scornful, cultured, hunch-driven boss. Their approaches couldn't be more different. They do however manage to solve one or two crimes.

I wonder if there's some relevance here for Dad and myself. I resolve to think on't. Though I have to admit I don't really know how to think about such things. What I do instead is wake up in the middle of the night and ruminate unhelpfully, getting myself into such a state that I wake Mr Mandy Sutter up too, and he offers to make me a cup of tea.

One thing though: if all Dad's seed potatoes come up, we're going to have one hell of a harvest later in the year.

Late June 2010. A new wheelbarrow

With things at the plot feeling chaotic, Mr MS and I do what couples often do when life feels unsettled and decide to become proud parents again. Not by getting another dog, but by purchasing a wheelbarrow that we hope will be safely delivered next week. It is a big step to take at the combined age of 105, but we are optimistic.

There was, however, some confusion when I rang the local hardware shop to order it.

'What's it made of?' I asked the bloke there.

'Green plastic,' he said. 'With a pneumatic wheel.'

'A what?'

'You know, a pumpy-up jobby.'

'Oh!' I said, surprised. 'Does the barrow come with a pump?'

'No. It comes with a wheel.'

Mr MS, standing beside me, looked puzzled. 'Is it an inflatable wheelbarrow?' he asked as I came off the phone. 'I've never heard of that before.'

'Nor have I,' I said, unsteadily.

But all is well. When the 'Bronco Bullbarrow' arrives, it is made of tough, forest green plastic. The wheels are smart red metal with a black tyre.

Many of the other barrows on the allotment site look a bit past it. Some of them look as though they have spent years upside down. They have rusty holes and wonky wheels.

This makes me feel extra proud of our new barrow, which carts things about a treat, barrelling jauntily along on its pumpy-up wheel. One of its greatest qualities is its ability to stand totally still. It reminds me of Dog MS: one minute alive in every sinew, the next comatose.

Before this, my only contact with wheelbarrows was when a friend persuaded me to take revenge on an ex. We put his phone number in the local paper, offering a free red wheelbarrow ('excellent runner') to the first person who called. We also offered his new cream sofa and a cockatiel complete with cage and accessories.

But I digress. I now have only one worry: what Dad will think. Dad, you see, got rid of all his garden paraphernalia when he and Mum moved up North, as the flat had no garden. He is prone to saying things like, 'that was a lovely wheelbarrow I had at the old place. I should never have got shot of it. What a waste! Of course, I had no idea then that I'd be getting an allotment!'

The delight of the second thought goes some way towards cancelling the sadness of the first, but not all the way. So out of respect I have been trying not to use the word 'wheelbarrow' in front of him, let alone talk about buying one. Let alone admit that I have actually bought one.

At his flat for weekly fish and chips though, I finally work up the nerve and tell him. He looks stricken. 'I suppose the day had to come,' he says. 'Where did you get it?'

Knowing that I am making things worse, I name our local (and rather expensive) hardware store. His chip-laden fork stops half way to his mouth. 'A bit pricey then,' he says, with narrowed eyes.

'Oh, it's only a plastic one,' I say, my voice sounding insubstantial, 'and it was reduced!'

This is true. It had £10 knocked off. It was still £41.99 though. I stuff my mouth with fish.

'How much was it?' asks Dad.

I take a big slug of wine. '£31.99,' I say. I feel bad. Giving a specific wrong figure is surely a sin of commission, not omission. But Dad mishears me. In that case, is it still a lie? I resolve to ask Mr MS later.

In the meantime, Dad is jubilant. '£21.99 for a plastic wheelbarrow?' he jeers. 'They saw YOU coming!'

Early July 2010. Weed killer

One day I realise that we've had the allotment for several months without resorting to weed killer. Dad fondly believes that the plot only takes an hour to clear and I have a vague prejudice against chemicals and hope all the bending and stretching involved in weeding will make me lose weight. But after weeks of pulling up the same weeds from what seem to be the same places, I'm beginning to think weight loss is overrated.

Then I go to Spain for a week and while I'm away the British weather offers perfect conditions for all the little weeds left on our plot to grow six feet high.

I find this out the moment I get back. I always ring Dad the minute I'm through the front door, as he worries so much about me travelling. But his greeting, though heartfelt, is brief. 'That allotment has turned into a right mess while you've been away,' he says. 'There's weeds all over the shop. What are your plans?'

I stare at my case, still unpacked. I haven't even seen Mr MS yet. I feel overwhelmed, which is probably why my mind goes immediately to one thing. 'Weed killer,' I say.

Then I remember: the allotmenteers in the new section of the site are middle class, unlike the rest. Therefore, we approve only of chemicals that biodegrade as soon as they touch the soil. 'Roundup,' I qualify.

'Oh, you don't want to go spending money on that rubbish,' says Dad. 'I've got some old stuff you can use.'

I don't like the sound of this. 'What's it called?'

'Oh, it hasn't got a NAME. It's just initials. Z's and X's. Letters from the arse end of the alphabet.'

'Is it eco-friendly?'

'You what?'

'Is it kind to the soil?'

'Of course it isn't kind!' says Dad. 'It's poison. But what does that matter? I might drop dead tomorrow, for all you know.'

I'm beginning to realise that this is Dad's way of saying 'whatever'.

'And so might you,' he adds, for good measure.

I decide I'd better go straight round. Mr MS is at work, anyway.

The stuff is in sachets inside an ancient black and red box. We go down to the plot and mix it in my pink watering cans. It's a dark, cloudy grey, with what looks like iron filings floating in it.

'There!' says Dad, 'I knew this stuff would come in handy one day.'

He teeters off over the tussocky ground and sprinkles the evil potion over our plentiful clumps of weeds. Nettles are the ones I recognise but there are other undesirables too. I force him to leave one clump of nettles, as I've been told they're a Good Thing in Moderation. Then as advised, we settle in for a ten day wait.

That night I toss and turn and when I finally sleep I dream that weed killer has seeped into the water supply and killed all the children at the primary school across the road from the allotments.

Mr MS has to make yet another of his 3am cups of tea. 'I think you're taking this too seriously,' he says. 'Anyway, he's only got six sachets. That's only enough to take out one small pupil group.'

I try to relax. Whatever the stuff is, it can't be that lethal. And if it is, I'll just have to lie to the other allotmenteers when their crops die. They won't be able to pin it on us, anyway. Especially as we've done it mid-week when there was no-one around.

As it happens, when Dad and I walk to the plot when the time comes, other people's crops look fine. I breathe a sigh of relief.

Reaching our plot though, I gasp. It looks as though it has been torched. Where there were tall swaying stems with green heart shaped leaves, there are blackened stalks with grey tatters hanging from them. I didn't know you could feel sorry for a nettle. The other weeds also look jolly poorly. The grass path looks burnt where the evil poison must have dripped from the can. My spinach and kale look okay, as do the little green sproutings that may be incipient turnips, but I dread to think what toxins they may have absorbed.

Even Dad looks shaken. 'Well, it's done the trick but it's a shame about the grass. Perhaps I shouldn't have made it up double strength. Only I thought it looked a bit weak.'

Later that evening, he rings. 'I've been thinking. We won't use any more of that stuff on the plot.'

I am delighted, not least because Dad is for once fighting his mania for using everything up down to the last drop, no matter how aged or unsuitable. I had a bout of food poisoning last year from eating some date expired Tesco's trifle at his flat.

He goes on. 'You can do the weeding by hand, can't you? Might help you lose a bit of weight. Besides, it only takes an hour to clear the plot.'

'Not even that long,' I say.

Mid July 2010. Good fences make good neighbours

Now that most of us new allotmenteers have equipped our plots with sheds, benches, barrows and varying amounts of vegetable seedlings, the focus on site shifts to fences.

The fences that surround the site as a whole are jolly sturdy. They are made of heavy gauge wire mesh. But they have a gap underneath which runs to six inches in places, so don't deter rabbits. They don't deter Jack Russell terriers, either, or people outside the allotments making smart arse remarks. Sometimes it's a Jack Russell owner who makes the smart remark and then it's a double whammy. Our plot being next to the river path and its walkers, we cop for it regularly.

One sunny day I arrive at the plot and am pleased to see Dad there, kneeling at the back in his shirt sleeves and work trousers, faded cream, as old as the hills and as familiar to me as anything. He is applying chicken wire to the bottom of the external fence to close the gap and has gone half way along already. When he stands up, I can see he's in a bad mood.

'I've not been able to get on at all this morning,' he grumbles. 'The number of people who've stood there gassing on the other side of the fence...! I had to tell one of them to bugger off.'

I tense, being the sort of person who worries excessively about falling out with others. But the comments can annoy. 'Rather you than me,' is a common one. They also like to talk, with relish, about the flooding and the rabbits. They don't need to tell us about the rabbits, who we are all beginning to recognise as a real pest, emerging nightly from their vast warren of underground chambers on the Yorkshire Water site next door to feast on people's pea plants. My spinach, kale and little turnip shoots are surviving, being foods that rabbits apparently don't like, but some cabbage seedlings I put in vanished overnight, like a conjuring trick. As for the flooding, a winter phenomenon, we'll have to wait and see.

31

I put my bag down on the bench. Dad chunters on. 'Of course they're all idiots, who can't see when a fellow's got a job to do.'

He unrolls chicken wire. His snow-white comb-over flops into his eyes and he pushes it aside. 'They're the sort who probably wear gloves to garden in.'

I delay extracting my own gardening gloves from my bag. 'Oh well,' I say. 'I'm sure they mean well. I'm sure they're just being friendly.'

I often say things like this to Dad, like some sort of promoter for the general public. I sicken myself. I sicken Dad too. 'Oh, you're sure of that, are you?' he snaps, attacking the wire with his cutters. But after a few minutes of silence he relents. 'It's not all bad, I suppose,' he says. 'One of them was a decent enough chap. Had an allotment here way back when. Seemed to know what he was talking about. Said that the floods don't do the soil any harm. Might even do it some good, what with the river silt.'

'If you want to talk to people, garden,' he adds.

I nod. Before the allotment, Dad had sometimes gone for days not speaking to a soul and had complained that he was forgetting how to talk.

I glance around the site. Fences have been going up everywhere. Trenches have been dug around plots and chicken mesh stapled to thick posts. Dad has vetoed the idea of fencing our plot. He thinks we should just put chicken wire around individual crops. 'Too bloody expensive otherwise. I mean, you don't want to start forking out serious money. That's not the idea, is it?'

A plot neighbour who always wears a leather cowboy hat comes over for a chat. He agrees with Dad about avoiding expenditure and tells us he has decided only to grow things that rabbits dislike. 'Rhubarb,' he says. 'Broad beans.' 'Courgettes,' I reply. We have obviously both been doing our homework. The man adds that he has written to the parish council suggesting that they supply a rabbit proof fence around the whole site. 'Huh. Good luck with that,' says Dad, rather vehemently, and goes back to his task.

As if to prove that at least one of us is friendly, I go on chatting to the cowboy hatted man for a lot longer than I want to. I discover that he could talk the hind leg off a donkey, let alone a rabbit.

At home later, Mr MS says he thinks fences are a good idea. He quotes sociologist Richard Sennett, saying that barriers help strangers stay cordial. But I realise I stand with the American poet Robert Frost, who says, 'something there is that doesn't love a wall.'

And it doesn't take long for Mr Frost to be proved right against Mr Sennett.

The following week, one allotmenteer leans over his new fence to strim away some edge vegetation on his neighbour's plot that he regards as weeds. The neighbour is furious, saying that the first man has trespassed and that these are wild flowers taken from his late aunt's garden.

'I was only trying to help,' the first man says, but the row escalates, with the neighbour threatening to set light to the other man's shed then saying that the whole allotment thing has been ruined for him now. Would this have happened if the boundary between plots was softer? I doubt it.

'Such passion!' says Mr MS when I tell him about it. Of course he can't imagine anyone getting worked up about vegetation of whatever kind. Once, when a driver fell asleep at her wheel and ploughed into our front garden, taking half our hedge with her, his first thought was not, 'Oh no, our hedge! And the amelanchier has been mown down too!' but, 'Is anyone hurt?' Incredible.

Also, he would never fall out with anyone at the allotments as his belief in courtesy dictates that he treat everyone with equal friendliness and stop for a longish chat wherever possible, especially when sent back to the car to fetch a spade that means he'll have to do some digging.

As for Dad, everyone at the allotments thinks he's marvellous so he can probably get away with being as friendly or as unfriendly as he likes. 'How is your father?' people ask continually. 'Fancy getting an allotment at age 87! They don't make them like that anymore.'

I can only agree: they don't.

Early August 2010. Watering

For a true gardener, I'm told, there's no such thing as bad weather. I ponder this one weekend as Mr MS and I sit in a Welsh field watching water pour glutinously down the windows of our camper van. At least the plot will get watered, I think, remembering long hot hours the previous week spent carrying water to parched ground over considerable distance. But it's hard to focus on this benefit when living at close quarters with a sodden beast. Not to mention Dog MS.

We get back and I discover that in Yorkshire it has hardly rained at all. Did I mention the distance between the allotment tap and our plot? It's 250 yards. That's five greenhouses, one set of pygmy goats, one twenty-foot hedge topiarised to look like the *Arc de Triomphe* and the sight of three allotmenteers on the established bit watering their engorged produce with hosepipes.

The chore is made worse by being a solo job, as Dad, now turned 88, can't walk easily on rough ground and even if he could, hates the watering cans I bought. 'I wouldn't be seen dead with those, love,' he says. Admittedly they are small and pink with black spouts. As a child I remember Dad refusing to ask a shop assistant for the ice cream I wanted because it was called a Love Heart and buying me a choc ice instead. 'Would you rather I got shot of them Dad,' I ask, 'and buy some green ones?'

'Have you got money to burn?' he snaps. Sometimes you just can't win. But I suppose, compared to a lot of other people, I have got money to burn. So has he. But as I've no doubt mentioned before, he doesn't like spending it. His last purchase was a spade from Poundland and even then he negotiated a discount because the handle was loose. He doesn't like me spending either, even though I've earnt it myself by the sweat of my own keyboard.

So we stick with the pink cans. At least Mr MS is willing to do the pink run. Annoyingly, this has enhanced his reputation at the allotments rather than detracted from it. Lady allotmenteers clamour to fill his can with their hoses.

But I'm not too bothered about produce this first year. I regard our plantings as an experiment. Apart from Dad's vast army of potato plants, we only have spinach, kale and turnips. I've popped in some globe artichoke seedlings for their 'architectural' qualities but am not expecting to dine on them. I've eaten some forkfuls of early spinach, a tiny amount that became tinier still when cooked, but I was chuffed to little mint balls. Anything that happens from now on is a bonus. Perhaps for once, my and Mr MS's low expectations of life are a blessing. A cup of berries? God bless you, squire.

The other plot holders don't share our attitude. The air fair bristles with a sense of middle-class entitlement. Although I can be described as middle-class myself, and so can Dad and Mr MS because they went to University as mature students (Mr MS studied philosophy and don't we know it) I feel we're not from the same milieu as the other plot holders. They have been demanding to know when the new tap to serve our section is being installed.

© JANIS GOODMAN 2020

But their pressure on the parish council bears fruit: men with metal detectors arrive and find the water main. It is under the plot next to ours! They dig a deep rectangular hole and put a red stick in it. We rejoice, briefly. But the stick proves to be a red herring as well as a red stick. When the tap appears the following week, it's as far from us as it could be without being in the next town. The cowboy-hatted man resorts to filling large plastic drums with water and rolling them to his plot. Mr MS reflects on the nature of civilisation and how humankind has always endeavoured to move water away from the places they don't want it and towards the places they do. And Dad, who would like to tell the Council to stuff their tap and the £17.50 a year they propose to charge for it, carries on researching a water pump to dredge the river running tantalisingly close to our plot. So far, including generator and ground works, the estimated project cost stands at £2,500.

Late August 2010. Rules and regs

Time is getting on and we still haven't officially signed for out plot. The council were slow sending out the contract and Dad is even slower in agreeing to sign it. He thinks he may want to challenge some of its clauses.

At his flat one morning he lays it out on his coffee table (a home-made item, painted with yacht varnish so that it shines like a conker in the leonine late summer sunshine) and says, 'Listen to this. The plot passes back to the Council 'on 1st January in the year next after the death of the Tenant.' I suppose that's alright. I might stagger on till the end of the year. On the other hand, I might drop dead tomorrow.'

I wait for the next part of this sentence. He doesn't disappoint. 'But then, so might you.' He has reached an age where the old jokes are the best, and improve with repetition. If it is a joke, that is.

'The thing is,' he goes on, 'we might end up doing a load of hard graft just for some other bugger to cash in on it.' He hands me a faded looking letter, typed on his ancient computer and printed off on an even more ancient dot matrix printer.

In it he says all of the above, more politely and therefore in a lot more words, to the Parish Council. He also claims that his health has deteriorated during the exceptionally long wait for a plot and asks whether his daughter may sign the agreement instead of him or if we can sign it jointly.

This is a shock for all sorts of reasons, but primarily because I didn't know that his health had deteriorated. 'Are you feeling ill, Dad?' I ask.

'No,' he says. 'But those buggers don't have to know that.'

I'm unhappy about him tempting fate. But I hand him the letter back to sign. Of course, my other reservation is that I'm not sure I want joint tenancy.

But then, when did Dad ever consult me about anything? He's certainly not about to start now.

A week later a letter comes back. Dad produces it over fish and chips. The Council is saying no. A strict rule forbids 'inheriting plots.' The unlawful felling of the ash tree is fresh in the Council's mind, so they throw in another ticking off about that too.

I'm surprised at how nettled I feel, considering that only a paragraph ago I wasn't sure I wanted joint tenancy. 'The bastards!' I say, chip laden fork descending.

Dad shrugs and munches on battered haddock. He seems unfazed. 'If I'm on my deathbed any time soon,' he says, 'I'll try and hang on till 2nd January. At least that'll give you another year.'

Mr MS sips his tea. 'Or we could have you embalmed,' he says, 'and prop you up inside the shed. No-one would know.' Dad sprays chewed fish all over the table. Sometimes Mr MS goes too far.

But as far as Dad is concerned, the matter is closed. It's his daughter who can't let it lie. Transferring the agreement at the outset, she thinks, can't be described as 'inheriting.' It's a technicality: if Dad had known the rule beforehand, he would've applied for the plot in joint names. She decides to tackle the Council herself.

The Council offices are opposite the station in our little town, in an imposing gritstone building. Their motto, translated from the Latin, is 'through health, wealth.' It harks back to the Victorian era, when we were a spa town. In modern days, it could relate to all the alternative health clinics and gyms here. It could certainly incorporate vegetable growing.

I enter the Parish Clerk's office prepared, having memorised my points and abandoned my normal work-at-home outfit of stained tracksuit bottoms and towelling dressing gown in favour of skirt and jacket. The equally smartly dressed woman before me doesn't answer any of my points however, but uses the broken record technique, repeating the phrases 'long waiting list' and 'can't make an exception' *ad infinitum*. 'All I can suggest,' she says at one point, 'is that you place your own name on the waiting list for another plot.' 'Hard as nails,' Dad would say. Although there is something admirable about her firmness, my eyes fill with tears of frustration.

'It's just the thought of Dad dying and my having to give up the allotment so soon afterwards,' I say, my voice wobbling. 'And his shed, that he's put up and customised with lots of little shelves and things.' It is only as I speak these words that I realise their truth.

To my surprise, her face softens. She says, 'what I will tell you is this. We have to act on the information we're given. The name on the rent cheque doesn't always tally with the name of the tenant. We note discrepancies but we don't always have time to follow them up.'

I am taken aback. 'You mean...?'

She stands up to indicate that our meeting is over.

I thank her and leave, unsure whether I've understood or not.

When I get home, Mr MS is standing at the cooker making his signature dish (i.e. the only one he can make) of Spaghetti Bolognese. I relay a garbled version of the conversation.

He is clear. 'She's told you how it's done! When people pop their clogs, no-one tells the Council.'

'But I don't want to lie,' I bleat.

He shrugs. 'So you'll have to enjoy the allotment for what it is now then let it go.'

As I may have mentioned before, Mr MS is a big fan of reality and of explaining it to me. I pull a face.

'Well,' he says, 'it's that or the embalming fluid.'

I go off to lay the table. I suppose he has a point. But my feelings have surprised me: passion about the whole thing must have crept up on me unawares while I was digging out miles of nettle root. I don't like the proposed solution. There's nothing I can do though but accept it. For now.

Early September 2010. Protection racket

To distract myself from the council's painful rules about inheritance, I turn my attention to fighting a different sort of pest: the rabbits. Protecting crops on an individual basis is proving a bit hit and miss. I bobbed in some lettuce seedlings last week and fenced them with chicken wire. But the determined creatures bashed the whole makeshift arrangement down and gobbled the lot. Having read that rabbits dislike human hair, Dad has sprinkled some of his snow-white clippings around the plot, but that doesn't seem to be helping either.

Growing crops that rabbits don't like, while successful up to a point (the kale, spinach and turnips are now nibbled, but only partially) has begun to seem limiting.

Other plot holders, fenced and unfenced alike, have been going for things that rattle on sticks. The site fair bristles with Benecol, Actimel and Yakult pots. I've often wondered what that stuff was for. Old CDs and DVDs are popular too, strung between poles. Paul McKenna's 'Overcome Emotional Spending' and the first series of 'Coast' swing between broad beans and further down, light glances off the rim of David Attenborough's 'The Life of Mammals: Meat Eaters.'

On the old part of the allotments stand two scarecrows. On one plot a stuffed character from South Park is hoisted aloft by a pole up his jacksie. The pole is sturdy, so when the wind blows nothing moves. It's hard to see how it would scare birds, though it does scare Mr MS. Then there's the Rastafarian. He doesn't move much either, just stands taking the breeze all day, though his fingers, made of plastic bags, stir occasionally. Mr MS finds much in him to admire. While Dad doubts that either of these gentlemen deter rabbits, I'm not so sure. The crops on their plots look pretty healthy.

On the new part of the site we're also encountering tiny beetles that turn crop leaves into doilies. The beetles, apparently, were disturbed by the

42

earthworks when the land was turned into allotments. Word is that they will 'settle down' next year.

'Has anyone told the beetles that?' asks Dad when Mr MS and I are round at his flat for coffee one Saturday.

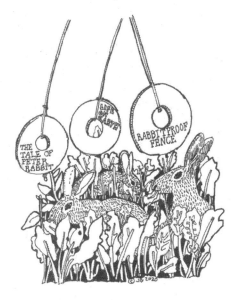

Mr MS nibbles at one of the Jacob's Orange Club biscuits that are endemic at Dad's flat. 'The Council could put up one of their strongly worded notices.'

I fail to laugh. I have some bad news for Dad. 'You know the woman next door to us?' I manage.

'The one that put her shed up on those ridiculous stilts?' asks Dad.

'Yes. Well, she's asking you for thirty quid. She's hired a company to put a rabbit proof fence around her plot tomorrow and it'll run down one side of ours.'

As I slurp my coffee, my shoulders creep to my ears, ready for a loud noise. They aren't disappointed.

'Hired a company?' explodes Dad. 'Christ! That's the wrong idea entirely!'

I launch into an explanation about our plot neighbour being a single woman with a full-time job. Her Dad might have helped her, I say, but he's in hospital. My motives for this speech are cloudy. It's as if I believe that fence-putting-up is the sole preserve of males and furthermore that they are all capable and willing to do it. Laughable. Dad isn't listening anyway. 'Surely she has a, err, male companion who could help?'

'Apparently not,' I say and wonder for a moment whether Dad's going to offer. 'She's paying the company £240,' I add.

'Good God!' Dad bangs his mug down. I am making things worse. I'm scared he'll refuse to pay and allotment relationships will be soured.

'It's ludicrous,' he says. 'I could have fenced her whole plot for thirty quid. Or thereabouts.'

I glance at Mr MS but he has immersed himself in his chocolate biscuit. An idea forms. I will pay her myself. Why didn't I think of that before? What an idiot! I wouldn't have even had to mention it to Dad. I begin to talk him down. 'Don't worry about it Dad,' I say. 'I'm sure she won't insist.'

But he surprises me. 'Oh, I'll pay up love, don't worry about that. I just can't get over the idea of paying someone £240 to fence a bloody allotment.'

A few days later, Dad hands over the money and during the week a fence appears on our party boundary. Dad examines it and pronounces it a load of bloody rubbish, though not in our neighbour's hearing.

He seems thoughtful. The next day, he rings up. 'Guess what? I've just been out for a spin. I found the place that manufactures the chicken wire for B&Q. I got a great roll of it cheap.'

'Well, great. But what for, Dad?'

'What do you mean, what for? Our fence, that's what for!'

He goes on. 'We don't need bloody great fence posts. It's only an allotment. Reckon I've got some old battens that will do. And we don't need a gate, do we? We'll just step over the fence. It won't be that high.'

44

I stare out of the kitchen window at our own garden gate, which is painted bright yellow and is one of my favourite things about the garden. I would have liked the excuse to paint a new gate and screw a brass number to it. But Dad is on a roll now and anyway it's great news that we're going to have a fence.

'I'm going down there now,' he says. 'I'll be in touch.'

Two days later our fence is up. Mr MS, Dog MS and I go down so Dad can show us his handiwork. Chicken wire stretches all the way around our plot, held up at intervals by thin but firmly secured battens. It is flimsy compared to other fences, which have thick fence posts, some set in concrete, and gates with latches. I have a dodgy knee at the moment and feel nervous about having to step over the fence onto uneven ground. But I can hardly complain about that to an 88-year-old man. And the fence is certainly serviceable. 'Thirty-eight quid all in,' he says. 'You can't beat that, can you?'

'You certainly can't,' says Mr MS, helping me over the fence. Dog MS clears it like a gazelle and we all sit down on the bench and a folding chair to enjoy the safety of our new, secure domain.

I gaze about me. There are no scarecrows yet on the new part of the site. So while it's true that I can't beat Dad's fence, I may be able to complement it in my own way. The nights will soon be drawing in, off-site tasks will have to be contemplated and it is high time the allotments had a female scarecrow. And who cares whether she scares any pests away? The point is, she'll look fantastic.

Mid-September. Where there's muck there's Mr MS

One mellow early autumn day, a chap with 'Mr Muck' painted on his van delivers a gently steaming pile to a common area on the old part of the allotments. I make enquiries. 'Ah, manure belongs to t'bloke in blue pickup,' says a chap with a tartan thermos flask. 'Ee'll likely let you 'ave some for nowt.'

This sounds excellent but it's tricky trying to pin down specific people at t'allotments, especially now it's autumn. People don't spend as much time there and even if they do, seem not to know anyone else's name or plot number (or perhaps they do, and won't tell us until we've been there 50 years).

''Im that puts up all t'fences,' is all you get about one man, while another is described as 'the goat man.' I wonder what names Dad, Mr MS and I go by. Dad could be 'auld gimmer in t'flat cap' though then again that describes half the allotment population. I've heard Mr MS referred to as 'that chatty lad,' even though he is nearly 60. I don't suppose I'll ever find out what they call me, unless it's 'that reet belter wi' t'flowing nut brown locks.' Anyway, I visit the allotment every day for a week but never see a man in a blue pick-up. I imagine him though, stripped to the waist and wearing tight denims, roll up drooping casually from his bottom lip.

I could just tek some of the muck wi'out askin' but I'm wary of annoying anyone in the old section of the allotments. As an incomer, a woman and clueless, I'm three points down already. Plus, us newbies have things to prove and I don't want to let the side down.

I decide to explore other avenues. I've seen a lamp-post in a nearby village that says 'Bagged Muck Available, FOC.' So I ring the number and the woman who answers says 'muck'll be out later.' I'm to turn right at the lamp-post and drive down a ginnel between a stone wall and a house to find it 'behind the red van.' Another instance of no name, no pack drill. I thank her profusely in my suddenly ludicrously middle-class voice.

That evening I drive down a pitch-dark alleyway and identify some bags of something by an old van that may or may not be red. The bags stand open, and as I lift the first one into the car I realise they are filthy and incredibly heavy and that I should have worn flat shoes and dirty old trousers.

I load most of them, cracking my head on the boot of my hatchback and getting black stuff on my Hobbs jacket. A 4 x 4 towing a caravan arrives behind me, from which a man dismounts and silently hoists the last bag into my boot. I begin to thank him but he holds up his hand to stop me and disappears into the house.

On the passenger seat of my car are the cans of lager I'd brought, a note taped to them saying THANKYOU. It seems all wrong to leave them now so I decide against it, the main thing being to avoid scraping the caravan as I reverse past it in the inky darkness.

The amazing thing is that the manure doesn't smell. I leave it in my car for a week before I take it to the plot. During that time I drive a friend all the way to the next town and back without her suspecting a thing.

As designated 'filth man' in our house, Mr MS deals with the bins, Dog MS's rear, the gunk that collects in plugholes and fishing things out of the toilet while I stand in a corner retching. So it's only fitting that he should help me with the horseshit.

On a damp but sunny day I drive him to the allotments. He hefts the bags from my car to our new wheel barrow and pushes it to the plot in a couple of loads. I think he's going to knock off with some spurious excuse, but to my amazement he stays and we upend the first bag onto the soil. We peer at it. 'It doesn't look very well-rotted, does it?' I say.

'It looks like turds mixed with straw,' he says.

But it's too late now. We spread it around the fruit bushes. Later, when he hears what we've done, Dad will say, 'I shan't be eating any blackcurrants this year, then.'

We dig the rest of it into the beds. Mr MS's blue handled fork is a blur. When we finish, the soil looks gorgeous, like broken up chocolate cake. Or broken up chocolate cake with turds in, anyway.

47

We lean on our forks. I survey our crops: the kale plants look very healthy despite having been nibbled by the rabbits before the fence went up. The turnip plants look as though they have now formed little turnips. I'm happy in a lovely uncomplicated way. 'You can keep your romantic dinners,' I say to Mr MS. 'This is my idea of a date.'

He laughs. He thinks I'm joking. But who needs the man in the blue pick-up?

October 2010. The chain of command

As autumn gets into chilly swing, it's still unclear who is in charge down at the plot. It certainly isn't Mr MS, who has restricted himself solely to following orders. He has held off from any major practical contribution too (though surely making a substantial philosophical one) having worked out that if he helps once a month, he can stave off any major criticism.

Unfortunately, the self-assembly bench he put up six months ago proves suspect. Dad and I are down at the plot one Saturday, planting overwintering broad beans and giving the manured beds another digging over (me) and erecting a compost bin out of old pallets (Dad). He's had another go at digging his potatoes but like last month and the month before there's little to show for his legions of plants and he has decided to leave them in to germinate again the following year. The plot has a wintry feel and damp clay clings to the spade. When we sit on the bench, there's a loud crack and we drop a few inches, though not completely to the ground.

Dad is surprisingly calm. 'Well, what do you expect when you buy a bench for £35?'

He sets to work immediately with the screws, tools and small Toblerone-shaped pieces of wood that are his stock in trade. The bench is rescued.

'Brilliant job, Dad!' I say.

'It's adequate,' he snaps. 'No more than that.'

Praise grates on him at the best of times and I suppose I sound gushing. But to me it is brilliant to be able to mend a broken bench so quickly and thoroughly. I say no more and content myself with sitting on the bench again and enjoying a feeling of security. Then I go back to my digging and save my hurt feelings to take out on Mr MS later.

The opportunity comes more or less immediately. Home and caked in mud, I find him lying on the chaise longue reading the Saturday papers. 'Your bench snapped in half!' I say by way of greeting. 'Dad had to mend it. Are you going to put preservative on it?'

Mr MS, a driving instructor in his spare time, reacts to danger by slowing down. He makes languorous hand movements. 'It's on the list.'

I know 'the list' for the passive aggressive tool that it is. But I realise I don't really want an argument – I want a bath. I settle for the last word. 'Well, it needs doing soon, with the bad weather on the way.' Later, Mr MS, ever the tactician, says that actually the job had been on his mind and he intends putting in an hour on it tomorrow. I am mollified and make sausage and mash for tea.

After tea, I ring Dad and tell him our plans for the bench. He is dismissive. 'Doesn't need treating. It's made of hardwood. Should go a nice silvery grey in time.'

'Oh,' I say. 'OK.' At least it means I can put Mr MS's proffered hour to better use. But the next morning, Dad rings back. 'I don't know why I was laying down the law about preservative. After all, it's your bench. Anyway, treating it will make it the same colour as the shed and that's no bad thing.'

I take this for an apology, and am touched. 'Dad seems fine whatever we do,' I say to Mr MS. 'So if it's up to me, I'd as soon you dug up some brambles.'

'Ok, foreman,' he says. It's his pet name for me.

He sets off in his wellies. But twenty minutes later, just as I am making myself a well-earned cuppa, he rings. 'Now, don't get arsey with me,' he says. 'But I'm going to have to go off and do a driving lesson. I got my timings mixed up.'

His voice is tinny on the mobile phone. I squish my teabag hard against the side of the cup. 'You don't have be Freud to work out that little slip!'

'No,' he concedes. 'But there is some good news.'

'What?' I bellow, holding the tea bag on the teaspoon.

'I did really enjoy those twenty minutes.'

'So you'll be going down there again soon then?'

'Oh! I...'

I glare at the phone, hoping he'll sense that he's one step away from a written warning. I lob the teabag into the bin.

'I suppose I could pop down tomorrow afternoon,' he says.

'Good,' I say, and hang up.

The next time Dad arrives at the plot, on a drizzly afternoon, and sees the bench, he shakes his head, incredulous. 'I don't understand why he hasn't painted that preservative on. What was he thinking about, leaving it untreated?'

I talk about brambles and priorities. 'Yes, yes,' he says, dismissive, and I realise he isn't listening to me at all; not even making a pretence of it. I also realise that his phone call before wasn't so much an apology as a change of

51

instructions. Suddenly I am furious. I don't mind him having a go at me, but having a go at Mr MS is different matter. 'He doesn't have to help us, you know,' I say, heated. 'He does have a full-time job.'

Dad stares at me open-mouthed. It is very unusual for me to 'talk back' – even as a teenager I rarely did. 'He puts a lot of effort in, considering it's something he's not in the least bit interested in,' I go on. I wave my hand at the shed. 'If you want the bench painting, you know where the preservative is. And the brushes.'

I stalk over to the other side of the allotment and lop the heads off some sopping wet nettles, then throw them onto the compost heap, stinging my hands to buggery. I am alive with anger and with the unusual sensation of having been honest. When I finally go back over to the shed, Dad seems unmoved and we talk about trivialities. I am desperate to apologise but manage to stop myself.

Later that evening, there's a phone call. I answer and Mr MS hears, from the kitchen, my sharply indrawn breath followed by a sob. 'I love you too, Dad,' I wail. We talk a bit longer, then I hang up and go into the kitchen and straight into Mr MS's arms.

'He's never said that to me before,' I sob. 'He waited until I was 53!'

'Better late than never,' says Mr MS.

I nod. It's hard to speak. It's not every day your world shifts on its axis. I've always known that Dad loved me. But to hear him say it is something else entirely.

November 2010. The river

The river that runs on the other side of our allotment back fence is described on Wikipedia as 'the most volatile and fastest rising river in the World.' The capitalisation of World may shake one's confidence in the author but it's true the river can rise and fall in moments, sweeping people off the stepping stones both further up and further down the river and even drowning them.

Folks who live near rivers like this know which areas flood and in what order. An excited Mr MS, back from his late-night walk with Dog MS, says things like 'the park's waterlogged but not the football pitch!' Or 'the path beyond the old bridge is now under water!'

Dad likes to talk about how he might get 'cut off.' Then he drives to Tesco's in Cheeky Looks and fills his boot with oranges, cartons of orange juice and packs of Jacob's Club Orange biscuits. Since retirement, his lunch has consisted of one banana and one navel orange. He likes his navels thin-skinned and if possible, slightly misshapen. He feels that these are the juiciest and he'll go to some lengths to hunt them down, even driving to other nearby towns. He won't tolerate oranges in a net, satsumas or thick skinned Jaffas, as Mr MS has found out to his cost.

But back to the river. The path walkers are divided on where exactly the floodwaters enter the allotments, just as none can say for sure what the land was used for before it became allotments. Some cock their eyebrows and say one thing; others shake their heads and say another. All, when pressed by a deranged-looking chap in a flat cap become more vague rather than less. So we allotmenteers don't know what to think. You've only to see our sheds, some on stilts, some flat to the ground, to realise that.

Bonfire Night comes and goes and as the nights draw in, it rains more often. One day it rains very hard and goes on for nearly a week. The river turns into a brown torrent. Tree trunks and bloated sheep hurtle past. Visitors and locals alike stop on all three bridges of our little town to take photos.

When the rain finally stops, I leave it a day or two then go to the allotments. The site is covered in mud. It's like seeing one's home after a burglary. The mind won't immediately interpret the visuals. 'Where's the DVD recorder?' it asks. 'I'm sure it was under the TV. Hey, where IS the TV? And why is the carpet covered in broken glass?'

On our plot, I wonder why bits of wood are strewn everywhere and why the bench is upside down. Why is a tub of creosote lying in the middle of mud-covered spinach? Where have the potato tops gone? Why are dead leaves heaped in drifts against the front fence and why are the three steps up to the shed (made by Dad out of plywood) black instead of light brown? When the penny drops, I phone Dad straight away. 'Well I never,' he says, sounding almost pleased. 'I'd better bring my new Wellies.' He drove 30 miles to buy these in a sale and has been dying to press them into use ever since. 'They make a heck of a lot of noise slapping the back of my calf,' he says about them as soon as he arrives, as if we are mid-way through a conversation. 'I keep turning round thinking some bugger's walking right behind me. But then what do you expect when you buy boots for £2.50?'

We begin the clearance. My job is to rake and bag mud covered leaves. Soon I too am covered in mud. Dad's job is to wonder that the water reached as high as it did, and check out every inch of the shed's interior for moisture. I glimpse once again the passion that can unite man and hut. 'Dry as a bone inside! What did I tell you?'

One of our neighbours arrives, a likeable young man with a toddler in tow. He built his shed flat to the ground and there is condensation inside his window. 'Did it get in?' Dad asks. 'Afraid so,' he says, removing the window to let air circulate. 'I'm not the only one, either.' He points to ground level sheds on other plots. They have also received interior soakings, judging by their windows. 'Sorry to hear that,' says Dad, hardly able to contain his delight. An hour or so later, as we walk back to our cars, he delivers his master stroke. 'I reckon our shed could do with raising a few more inches.'

I have absolutely no idea how this can be done. It sounds impossible. But next day when I meet Dad on site he is armed with four bricks and the pristine car jack from Cheeky Looks. Singlehandedly, he jacks the shed legs up one by one and inserts the bricks underneath. And so the shed goes up in the world. 'That should keep the weather out,' he says, straightening up. 'Good job, Dad,' I say and for once he doesn't contradict me.

Then I see he has cut a V out of the tops of both his Wellies and gaffer taped the edges together to make them fit. They look bloody uncomfortable. But customising them, I know, will have given him a lot more pleasure than buying a decent pair in the first place.

December 2010. Christmas shed

Dad enjoys our monthly trip to the local garden centre. It is warm with decent toilets, full of people his own age and you can walk for miles unobtrusively supporting yourself on a trolley. There's no stigma attached, unlike a Day Care Centre, and it's free, unlike a National Trust property.

One morning we walk through the Christmas decoration section. Fairy lights, strings of icicles and candles of every colour shimmer, twinkle and flick on and off in complex sequences. It sets him off on a rant. 'Who in their right mind would give THAT house room?' he explodes at a large glittery snowman with a black top hat. A huge Santa waves from an illuminated sleigh that goes backwards and forwards. 'Would anyone actually pay for a monstrosity like that?' he bellows.

A nearby family look sheepish so I urge him on into the next section. Bags of giant purple pot pourri, 'Meditainment' CDs and hexagonal jars of honey are not much of an improvement so I stride on into the tools section to find respite among tones of wood and metal.

Dad, however, is on a roll. He examines a garden fork. 'What kind of halfwit would buy this? It'll fall to pieces inside a week.'

He's probably right: real gardeners surely don't shop here, paying over the odds for concrete horses' heads and Big Drippa Automatic Watering Systems. Who needs a rain cover for their chiminea? And if they do, what's wrong with a black bin liner? The garden centre is indeed a temple to shopping, not gardening.

Nevertheless, we manage to spend three hours there. We wander about dissing things, go into the cafe for a coffee and a mince pie, do the Codeword in the free newspaper then spend almost an hour in the discount books section, which cheers Dad up no end. He picks up a glossy tome about bread making.

'Look at this!' he says.

'I didn't know you were interested in baking.'

'Never mind that. 452 pages and look at the quality of the paper! The thing weighs about a pound. Now that's what I call good value.'

By then it's time for a turkey and cranberry sandwich and another cuppa.

We call at the supermarket on the way home and take separate baskets. Knowing he'll insist on paying for my shopping, I decide just to buy a couple of items. I'll have to come back later anyway as I want something from the garden centre that I didn't dare buy in front of him.

Standing by shelves containing a baffling array of toothpastes, he watches me put three packs of Paracetamol in my basket. 'They won't let you buy that many,' he says. 'It's two per customer, in case you're a suicide risk. Ridiculous isn't it? Health and Safety gone mad.'

'Would three packs be enough to kill someone?' I ask.

'Oh yes,' he says. 'If you washed them down with a bottle of gin.'

I'm unsettled by his grasp of the subject. He goes on. 'But if that's what you were going to do, you'd do it anyway, wouldn't you? You'd just have to go to Sainsbury's AND Tesco's. They must think we're all imbeciles.'

I decide to leave the tablets in my basket to see what happens. Amazingly, the young woman at the till, with her black nail varnished fingers, checks them through without comment or interest. The till system doesn't stop her. I'm hoping Dad will be pleased but instead he's furious. He leans across the checkout and points at me. 'Now she's going home to commit suicide!' he shouts.

The young woman's mouth drops open.

'It's alright. I'm not really,' I say and laugh a jolly little laugh as though this is all a joke. Needless to say, I am blushing to the roots of my hair and can't get us out of the supermarket quickly enough. Dad is unperturbed and chuckles as we make our way back to the car. 'That showed her, didn't it?' he says.

Later, at the garden centre alone, I make my way back around all the items we viewed earlier. Sometimes when we're together it's as if I can't see things properly, let alone decide whether I want to buy them or not. I linger by the Big Drippa, taking it in. I begin thinking it might be useful for watering next year's seedlings when we go on holiday. But recognising the danger of knee-jerk rebellion expenditure, I pull myself together and head to the Christmas decorations section. I scoop up a large box of multicoloured fairy lights powered by a solar panel. If those aren't frivolous and unnecessary, I'd like to know what is. But I can just see them, down on the plot, festooning the shed in the gathering dark.

January 2011. Rabbit, rabbit, rabbit

Over Christmas and New Year, it is too cold for Dad to venture out so he doesn't see the fairy lights in situ. It snows on and off for 3 weeks and the lights, arranged around the shed door, glow unimpeded until Twelfth Night, when I take them down. Then the snow vanishes. We got used to its white blanket: I visit the plot one afternoon and notice how very brown and bare it looks. It's amazing how contrast affects the mind, I think, doing a Mr MS.

I glance around the plot and frown. Weren't my curly kale plants over there by the fence? Just where those brown woody stalks are now? I remember them green and sturdy, like little palm trees. With this being our first year, I hadn't expected much from them but they ended up delivering a good few portions of greenery, contributing to our 5-a-day all through December.

Well, they've gone. It gives me a pang. While it's best to be stoical about allotment ups and downs – as Rudyard Kipling says, 'You must watch the things you gave your life to, broken, and stoop and build 'em up with worn-out tools' – those neat attractive plants, that survived both flood and mud, were my favourites.

I think I know whodunnit though. A couple of weeks ago I saw tracks in the snow going up and down the paths and round and round inside most of the plots, even the ones with the sturdiest of fences. It was like an Enid Blyton crime scene. They'd left jobbies all over t'shop too, like the calling card of a particularly nasty psychopath.

I carry on with my plot inspection. The globe artichoke plants look okay as do (miraculously) the broad bean shoots that came through just before Christmas. The everlasting spinach is surviving too, probably because I pegged a fleece tunnel over it for protection. And in common with others of my acquaintance, rabbits obviously don't get hungry enough for turnips. Those are still lolling about our plot like purple faced boozers. I'm not surprised. Exciting though it was to see them grow, we haven't managed to actually eat that many.

Since there's no kale to pick, I go to see Dad for coffee. He greets me at the door wearing one of his Christmas presents from us: a black sweatshirt printed with the name Ted the Shed in white.

'You're wearing it!' I say. I wasn't sure he would. His eyes scan the pavement behind me. 'Come in, come in,' he says. 'I don't want any of the neighbours to see it. They might get the wrong idea.'

'The wrong idea about what?' I ask, following him up the steep stairs to his flat. 'I think it looks rather smart.'

'The lettering's a bit blinding,' he says and teeters off to the kitchen to make coffee. He has cut the tops off all his socks because they had grown tight and soft beige cotton concertinas around his ankles.

He made his coffee tray out of a piece of plywood. It has a shallow varnished rim and is lined with bright blue sticky backed plastic. It is just the right size for two mugs of coffee and two Jacobs Orange Club biscuits. He deposits everything on the coffee table (also homemade) and sits down with a sigh of relief. 'Well, I made it past 1st January. You've got the allotment for another year.'

'Great,' I say and tell him about the rabbits and about how they got into all the plots, even the substantially fenced ones. He is delighted. 'Just goes to show, you can spend all the money you like and it won't do you the slightest bit of good!'

We sip our drinks. He makes coffee at just the right strength, more than I can say for either Mr MS or myself because we guesstimate the coffee to water ratio. Dad measures it precisely, with a plimsoll line on the cafetiere and a plastic scoop he has cut down to exactly the right size.

'Anyway,' he says, 'we can afford to lose ten percent of our produce to rabbits.'

'Ten percent?' I say, remembering my vanished cabbage and lettuce. 'What if they forget their calculators?' It is the kind of joke he might make and he laughs. 'I asked everyone how high rabbits jump. But no-one knew. Well, now we do. How about catching a bit of news?'

Without waiting for an answer, he presses his remote and the screen of his gigantic TV flickers into brightly coloured life. He has an appetite for 24-hour news coverage, especially when there's a natural disaster on the cards. 'There's always some bugger worse off than yourself,' he says, gratefully.

The matter of the rabbits, I gather, is closed. I screw up some tissue, spit on it and stuff it into my ears to take the edge off the news drumbeat. While Dad's immersed in hurricane footage, my thoughts drift back to our allotment and the most recent lesson it has taught me: in winter, rabbits get hungry enough to eat even the plants they dislike.

February 2011. The Lady of Shallot

On Valentine's Day I finally get around to making my scarecrow. She is a raven bin bag haired beauty with a striped blouse and a statement necklace of shallots. But when I go down to the plot to install her, the ground is too hard. I decide to store her in the shed for a little while, until it's a bit warmer. But that's my story. She has her own take on things.

> On one side of the river lie
> Long beds of turnips and of rye
> ('tis used as green manure, that's why)
> And past KwikFit the road runs by
> From wint'ry Camallotment,
> Where gale-force winds and snowy showers
> Have killed off all the cauliflowers
> And where the silent shed imbowers
> The Lady of Shallot.

> Only the postie, walking early
> Down the river path to Burley,
> Hears a song that echoes cheerly
> From the nearest shed quite clearly,
> Across be-wintered Camallotment:
> And by the moon, dogwalkers weary,
> Bagging turds in uplands airy,
> Listening, whisper, 'Tis the fairy
> Lady of Shallot.'

There she sits by night and day
Waiting for winter to go away.
She heard the one who made her say
Her looks will fade if she should stray
out onto frozen Camallotment.
One knows not what the weather may be,
And so she sits there steadily.
But cooped-up in the shed feels she,
The Lady of Shallot.

Through the window most unclear
In this, the winter of the year
Men in flat caps do appear
And there she sees the A65 near
Winding down to Camallotment:
There the river eddy whirls,
And there the surly council-churls,
And tail of Dog MS unfurls
Outside on Camallotment.

And then one day near her shed-eaves,
Some tools from out a car are heaved,
And sun comes through the wych elm leaves,
And flames upon the brazen greaves
Of Sir MS Lancelotment.
Up to the shed he boldly stumbles
When asked to dig the earth he grumbles
'I can only stay an hour,' he mumbles,
'On this freezing Camallotment.'

His furrowed brow in sunlight glows
(On burnish'd tyres he usually goes)
Beneath his baseball cap there flows
His greying hair, and rose-red nose
On perishing Camallotment.
From the bank and from the river
The cold air really makes him shiver
'It's brassic by this bloody river,'
Sings Sir MS Lancelotment.

She leaves her seat, she's lost her head,
She hops three paces thro' the shed,
A knight like this she'd planned to wed
And take unto her turnip bed
On forsaken Camallotment.
But down she falls and flat she lies
The window cracks from side to side;
'I forgot I wasn't real!' sighs
The Lady of Shallot.

In the stormy east wind straining
On other plots, the workers waning
The broad stream in its banks complaining
Heavily the low sky raining
Over lonely Camallotment.
Bold Sir MS is quite a-flurried
'Has a bird got in that shed?' he worries
And to the padlocked door he hurries
To the Lady of Shallot.

And there she gives him quite a fright
Lying, robed in black and white
That loosely blows from left to right
Her skirt being made to catch the light;
Scare pests from Camallotment.
But undeterred he takes her hand
And as he brings her out to stand
He hears a craz'd humming sound
From the Lady of Shallot.

It's like a pop song, not quite holy
Chanted loudly, chanted slowly,
'By heck' he breathes and 'Holy Moly!'
And quickly pegs her in the lowly
Soil of Camallotment.
It's done. He puts his tools away
And lives to dig another day
Relief! It's been a bad spade day
For Sir MS Lancelotment.

But he'll get over it. Now she stands
Upon the Parish Council lands
In rain and snow and river sands
Holding sunlight in her hands
On chilly Camellotment.
And though the birds shit on her dress
And rain has made her face a mess
She wears the smile of someone blessed,
The Lady of Shallot.

By Alfred Lord Table-Tennyson

March 2011. High winds

The Lady is happy: we're all happy. As early spring arrives, she continues to lend the plot that much needed touch of glamour. But it's windy here in our valley, especially at this time of year. One night, the buffeting in our attic bedroom gets so bad that it's impossible to sleep. Prone to forecast disaster (a family trait) I toss and turn into the wee small hours. I'm concerned about the Lady and also about my globe artichoke plants, which have lots of new, tender looking stems, arching like splashing fountains of silver green. More pressingly, next door's chimney is cracked and I fear it will fall through our ceiling.

Mr MS is no help. Rather than shin up onto the roof and fix it there and then (my preferred option), he says things like, 'we had it looked at and the builders said it was fine. Why don't you put your earplugs in?'

Eventually I do. When I wake up, I'm delighted to find that a) it is morning and b) I'm still alive. I go down to the plot. The Lady is beaming: she seems to have found the wind exhilarating, though I have to tuck her skirt in again as it now leaves nothing to the imagination.

As for the globe artichokes, some leaves are broken but most are still intact, their edges like circular saw blades. When I've finished fussing at ground level however, slicing the damaged leaves off at the fleshy base and putting their fleece back on, it strikes me there's something wrong with the sky.

I stare upwards. It's like bumping into an old friend minus glasses or beard: it takes a few moments to figure out what's changed. But then I see: the usual tracery of branches and twigs overhead, so reminiscent of a diagram of the human central nervous system, is gone. The wych elm is down and lying prone.

I hurry over to it. Its roots are broken on one side and torn out of the ground on the other. Luckily it has fallen away from the shed. I gaze, remembering the notice the Parish Council pinned to it last year. DO NOT CUT

DOWN THIS TREE. The wind has obviously never learnt how to read. The tree is down whether the Council likes it or not.

I can't wait to tell Dad. But he opens the door to Mr MS and me that evening already beaming. 'Have I got news for you!' he says. Despite not having visited the plot all winter, he happened to go down this morning to get the wood preservative from the shed and saw the slain giant. I feel cheated, having looked forward to being the bearer of good news, for once.

'I've already drafted a letter to the Council,' he says. 'Anyway, come in.'

'Oh, there's no need to involve the Council,' says Mr MS, following Dad down the hallway. As usual he is innocent of the dark passions involved in his father in law's relationship with authority. 'I'll hire a circular saw at the weekend and cut it into timber.'

I stare. 'If only we could use the globe artichoke leaves to cut up the tree!' I say, which seems every bit as likely to me as Mr MS operating a circular saw.

But Dad turns. 'Don't you touch that tree!' he says, sounding a lot like the original notice would have done if it could speak. 'Don't so much as break off a twig. That tree belongs to the Council. It's up to them to dispose of it and that's what I've told them, in no uncertain terms.'

He speaks with the satisfaction of one who has lived long enough to see justice prevail. And he doesn't want his justice interfering with.

He is indeed so satisfied that even Mr MS, who thinks well of everyone, is suspicious. 'Did he poison it?' he asks on the way home in the car. 'Or blow it up?'

I think about the sachets of weed killer still in Dad's possession. I think of his expertise with explosives during his career as a seismologist. Everything adds up a little too neatly, including his visit to the plot following the tree's downfall, like a felon returning to the crime scene. Even so, I can't really imagine it. 'Surely not,' I say. 'Wouldn't he have told us if he had?'

Mr MS shrugs and pulls up outside our house. I glance up at next-door's chimney. You can't see the crack from here, but I know it's there. 'At least it isn't windy tonight,' I say. And at least that's it now, as far as the trees on our plot go. There are none left standing, so there are none to fell, be it by bow saw, bane or boom.

Early April 2011. The tarp

Gardeners, I'm learning, see things differently to normal people. An ordinary family meal is imbued with more tension than a Christmas episode of East Enders as I watch Mr MS boil to buggery the everlasting spinach nurtured all through the winter in a fleece tunnel. 'I can't eat that,' I cry. 'You've turned it into mush!'

Mr MS is wily creature. 'I'll eat it tomorrow. I like cold mush.'

As he well knows, I'm out tomorrow visiting a stately home with a friend, so whether he eats it or chucks it I'll never know. But I keep quiet. At least he's said something that saves face on both sides.

At the stately home, the slant view of the gardener resurfaces. Despite the fascinating history of the place, its 'Yorkshire Rose' windows and carved stone head of Charles I, my friend's and my interest is at best polite. When we get to the gardens though, emotions run high. The leaf shoots on the apple and pear trees look impossibly vivid and delicate against their damp dark bark. 'Oh! Oh!' cries my friend. 'It's no good, I'll have to move house. I MUST have an orchard.'

What arouses my passion is the compost heaps. There are four. Four! All at different stages of decay. We only have one, built last year by Dad out of old pallets. Next to the heaps is a chicken wire drum of dead leaves. I've heard tell of leaf mould and its soil-enhancing properties and this drum with its darkening coppery strata is a vision. I long for beauty like this on our plot. That night I hardly sleep. Yes, I know. But the leaf drum, easily installed the next day with wire and bamboo canes, is magnificent.

There's something else I long for. In Cormac McCarthy's post-apocalyptic tale, *The Road*, father and son walk a blasted anonymous landscape armed with little more than a tarpaulin to sleep under. Having listened to the audio book over winter, I heard 'the tarp' mentioned so often that I became

71

mesmerised by it. Never mind the searing insight into humans' capacity for good and evil that McCarthy offers, what I took from the book was the desire for a tarp. It would keep my compost heap warm.

Dad and I take our monthly trip to the local garden centre. In the plastic greenhouse section, Dad fingers a tarp then sings his signature tune. '£14.99 for a sheet of bloody plastic? You've got to be joking!' He enjoys complaining, I'm beginning to realise. And anyway, in his defence he hasn't read the book. Nor is he likely to. The garden centre has a camping section so we go there to see if the price of the groundsheets is more acceptable. It isn't. 'Let's go for a coffee,' I say. I can always come back another day. If I want to, that is. I half agree with him. But on the way out of the camping shop, I notice something interesting in the waste bin. I fish it out. It's a large piece of thick plastic that has obviously been used to wrap something big.

'Look at this, Dad!' I say. He grins. 'That's more like it.' We go back up to the sales desk. 'Can we have this?' We've already told the chap there about the allotment and my plans for the compost heap. 'That's £48 please,' he says.

'How much?' Dad's mouth falls open.

'Go on, tek it,' says the chap.

We deliver a shocked laugh and a thank you then scarper with our placcy prize before he changes his mind. In the coffee shop, we take a window table. 'Wasn't it nice of him to let us have it for nothing?' I say. My gratitude is genuine but I realise too late that yet again I'm trying to manipulate Dad into showing warmth towards his fellow human. Dad in his turn is always trying to temper my gullibility. He pulls a face. 'Makes you realise how much money they must be making on the ones they sell for £14.99.'

I sigh. 'I'll go and get the coffees, shall I?'

'Hang on a minute, love,' says Dad. 'We'd better have some lunch.' He extracts a roll of notes from his trouser pocket and peels off a twenty. 'Mine's a fish and chips. With garden peas. Have whatever you fancy. After all we've saved ourselves £14.99, haven't we?'

'Thanks Dad!' I say, feeling suddenly teary. I think of him as stingy. But he's not stingy about everything. Far from it. He bought Mr MS and me a top-notch DVD player for Christmas. 'Quality is worth paying for,' he said.

I join the queue at the counter. Lunch AND a tarp, I think. It doesn't get much better than that. What's more, we'll be alright when the apocalypse comes.

©JANIS GOODMAN 2020

Part 2 – The following year

Late April 2011. A good bushman

We begin our second calendar year of allotmenteering. There is no fanfare from Dad or Mr MS, but I decide to celebrate one Sunday by buying some 6' garden canes and going down to the plot to erect a bean tower. The main news there is that a) the tarp has been in place for three weeks and b) the fallen wych elm on our plot, as yet unattended by the Parish Council, is starting to attract attention.

The trouble is that it's close enough to the fence for passing male dogs to pee on. Passing male men would probably like to do the same but convention dictates that they can only eye it and ask questions. 'What happened to your tree?' asks one, stopping. His female companion, who has walked on ahead, turns and sighs.

'It fell down,' I reply, enjoying rewarding a dumb question with a dumb answer. I'm preoccupied with thoughts of whether beans would be safe from the rabbits if I surrounded them with a double layer of chicken wire. The loss of my kale plants in January still hurts.

The man brightens, as if I've said something interesting. He is wearing a cloth hat that begs for corks. He continues to hover. I relent. 'It blew down, actually,' I offer.

The woman frowns. She is probably wrestling with impatience. 'Why does he always have to TALK to people? Has he forgotten it's Sunday and Tesco's shuts at four?'

But the man goes on gazing at the fallen tree. It seems to exert a hold on him. The woman stands where she stopped. To drift back would be to condone his dawdling; to move on would be rude. Besides, her rationalisations will be kicking in now. 'I suppose it is HIS walk too. And his weekend off work. He's got SOME right to do what he pleases.'

I have to admit I'm on her side. If there were sides, that is. So I offer no further information. They might never get their pork chops and broccoli otherwise. Also, it's chilly and I'm busting to erect my bean tower. But I don't move away because what kind of miserable cuss can't stop for a word with a well-meaning passer-by? The three of us stand on, held in place by invisible force fields.

Then she glances at her watch and gives a little sigh. It's a move I admire. She has made herself clear without stooping to harangue him in public. The man, obviously adept at decoding her gestures, nods and steps away from the fence. He looks resigned. Then he makes an extraordinary remark. 'A good bushman, that's what you need. A good bushman would turn that tree into logs in no time.'

I am thrilled by this remark, conjuring as it does a vision of the Australian outback. I'm reassured to know that my sense of hat corks wasn't misplaced. My mind skips ahead. Perhaps the Council will indeed send a bushman, who will whittle some of the thicker twigs into little wooden animals, carve a slim branch into a flute and teach me to play a tune on it.

Later, a killjoy will tell me that a bushman is a kind of saw. But for now, I stand, lost in a dream. Then I realise that the couple has gone. I miss them. I liked the unexpected window on the world that they opened.

But thoughts of the Scarlet Emperors of the future are waiting to rush in and soon I am back where I belong: in the security of a more British fantasy, about vegetables.

The following day, someone does come from the Council. He snips a few leaves off the fallen elm and writes to Dad to say that it has been 'made safe.' Seems it's up to us to shift the main bulk of the thing, to chop it up and dispose of the wood. I break the news to Dad over the phone, thinking this will provoke him into firing off another of his letters. 'Fair enough,' he says. I blink. Before he took on this allotment, I'd have said I knew my Dad pretty well. But these days, I just can't guess what will incense him and what he'll take like a lamb. Mr MS sometimes surprises me too. When told the news, he mentions his circular saw plan again as if it is actually a reality.

In the event, Dad finds a suitable saw in his tool box and the following weekend, he and Mr MS form a two-man chain gang, with Dad sawing and Mr MS carting the logs to our camper van in the wheelbarrow. Dad doesn't appear to be pushing himself in a shit or bust manner, which makes the whole scenario more relaxing for idle bystanders like my good self. I am impressed. I feel disloyal that I wished for a bushman when, as it turns out, two bushed men can do the job just as well.

Early May 2011. A friend in weed

We stow the lovely logs in our garden shed for winter. Then Dad and Mr MS disappear from the allotment completely. Mr MS says he is busy with work (that old chestnut!) and Dad has a big project in hand. To address a recently increased incidence of 'funny turns' he has bought a blood pressure monitor and is taking his own readings many times a day, entering them on a huge spreadsheet and including detailed mitigating factors that he feels his GP may be interested in. When invited to the plot, he says, 'Hmm, I don't know. I've got a hell of a lot going on here.'

I sympathise. But a hell of a lot is going on at the plot also, mainly involving the exponential growth of weeds I thought we'd seen off for good last year. The whole shebang will need to be dug over and weeded anew. In Dad's absence (and even in his presence) I feel responsible for this. I do a lengthy stint digging up ground elder. The task is dispiriting: it feels like reinventing the wheel. Alone.

In the past, when I've mentioned the allotment to friends, they've said things like, 'Ooh, lucky you! How rewarding, eating your own veg. And all that fresh air and exercise!'

You would have thought then that they'd be keen to spend a day outdoors with me, digging. But no. Despite the benefits they list, when I ask for help their nostrils flare and they come up with a variety of wafer-thin excuses. Of course, it's no good asking friends who do have allotments, or even big gardens. All they're able to offer is a shoulder clasp in silent solidarity at this difficult time of year. But I have a friend whose kitchen wall I helped damp proof with bitumen ten years ago, the vilest act of DIY I have ever participated in. It is time to call in the favour. She grudgingly agrees to come round the following Sunday morning.

81

On the day, she turns up an hour late, badly hung over and in need of breakfast. I make her toast and coffee and assure her that the peace and tranquillity of the allotment will make her feel better. There is rarely anyone else down there, I say, and the sound of bird song is healing.

Unfortunately, when we finally get down there, a plot neighbour is drowning out all the birdsong by going at it with a petrol rotavator. 'Sorry,' he shouts above the din, 'but I've only got this contraption for ninety minutes so I'd better get on.' My friend shows great strength of character for the first five of these minutes, then says, 'I can't stand this. I need more coffee.'

When we return after three more coffees, our neighbour has gone and it is lovely and quiet. We begin clearing. To hand it to my friend, she does manage to turn a patch of soil to a fine tilth. Unfortunately, it is only two-foot square which, given the size of the allotment, is about as much use as a pastry spade. 'Look,' I say. 'Don't sweat the small stuff. Just get the big weeds out and give it a rough digging over.'

'Oh, but you know I've got a bad back,' she says. This is the first I've heard of any bad back. But it's a trump card. I mutter bitter condolences and turn back to digging out dandelion roots that go half way to Australia.

The following week when another friend volunteers to help, I'm not expecting much.

But this second friend announces on arrival that of all garden tasks weeding is her favourite because she loves to see cleared soil. And she works like a Trojan. We dig up nettle after nettle and rosebay willow herb after rosebay willow herb.

My friend seems to need no breaks. I offer her tea from the plastic mug I keep in the shed for visitors.

'I'd rather get on,' she says. Her work ethic is phenomenal. Or else she saw me empty the dead spider out of the mug.

An idea strikes me. 'Would you like to get more involved?' I ask. 'Take over part of the plot perhaps? Think how rewarding it would be, eating your own veg. And all the fresh air and exercise you'd get.'

She gives it two seconds' thought. 'Naah,' she says.

I console myself by making a bonfire.

It produces a smoke cloak that drifts east, enfolding the couple diagonally opposite. They move all around their plot to escape it and eventually leave, coughing.

'You should have let the damp stuff dry out first,' says my friend. 'Now, are you going to help me dig up the rest of this nettle root or not? That fire will keep going without you standing there watching it, you know.'

'Give me a minute,' I say. 'Did I ever tell you I've got a bad back?'

Mid-May 2011. The carp

With the weeding and digging largely done, I turn my attention once again to our compost heap. Superficially, it looks exactly as I think a compost heap should look. But it's time to check out the state of play sub-tarp.

Unfortunately, when I lift the lid, everything beneath it is dry as a crust. It has been an unseasonably warm spring and it looks as though the tarp has been doing its job too well and acting as a giant magnifying glass for the sun. Visiting worms and beetles must be finding it a bitter disappointment, like arriving at a half-built hotel. I throw a bucket of water on the heap and stow the tarp in the shed. As so often with this allotment lark, I will have to think again.

On the way out, I notice several carpeted heaps. Perhaps that's the way to go. It is old school, I know. The princess in me shudders at carpet's tendency to harbour slime and the disciples of slime. Then again, a year of trying to grow things has wrought a change in me. Before: 'Eww. Look at that soggy dirty carpet. How vile!'

Now (admiringly): 'That carpet is keeping the heap warm while allowing rain and air in and encouraging microorganisms to break the carbon-containing waste down through aerobic respiration!'

It seems I have begun to assess things by how they work rather than by how they look. If only this process had happened years ago! It would have saved me many painful mistakes in the romance department. And of course, function and utility are among Dad's highest values. Perhaps I am turning into him.

In the following days, I ask around and am told that natural fibres are the way to go. Over the next week on my travels here and there, I stop at many a promising-looking skip for a rummage only to find that a deplorable lack of quality has set in nowadays as regards home furnishings. All I can find is foam-backed carpet and some of it, found in a skip outside a local pub, looks as though it has spent several years atop a compost heap already.

Knowing that Dad still has rolls of pure wool carpet in his spare room from the house we lived in when I was eleven, I ask him if he can spare a small square of it. He is mortally offended. 'That's decent stuff, that is! You might be glad of that in a few years' time.'

The thought of that over-familiar swirly blue pattern covering the floor in any house I share with Mr MS makes me feel unutterably depressed and as if my life has come to nothing. But it's best not to say so. 'Yes Dad,' I say, 'you never know.'

I decide to try another tack. I go into an actual carpet shop in our small town and ask if they've any spare.

The chap serving shakes his head sadly. But a man leaning on the counter says, 'Scrap carpet? We've tons of the stuff at our warehouse. Tell my son his Dad sent you.'

He gives me directions to a place near a level crossing outside a nearby town. But because I think I know where it is, I don't really listen and end up crossing the border into Lancashire, a state of affairs that, as any inhabitant of Yorkshire will tell you, is regrettable.

I drive a bit more before admitting to myself that I am completely lost. Suddenly it is all too much. Tears prick my eyes. Why am I spending time and petrol on this wild goose chase? Composting – I'm through with it. What's wrong with buying a few sacks of it at the garden centre?

I decide to take the most direct route home. Of course, that's when I find the level crossing, and the carpet warehouse. I walk round the back and see a skip with a rug on top that looks exactly the right size.

Inside the shop, the lad behind the till confirms that I can have it for nowt. He also confirms that it's Axminster, with not a trace of manmade fibre in sight. I nearly hug him.

Down at the plot, the rug fits perfectly: the compost heap looks resplendent.

So now we are 'carp' rather than 'tarp'. The rug lets in the rain and I'm sure that the compost will soon be coming on a treat. It certainly should do, considering it now enjoys a higher quality covering than our living room floor.

Later May 2011. The chicken chatterer

The spell of good weather continues all through the month and we have some lovely sunny days. But Dad is still compiling his blood pressure dossier and is wary of doing any work at the allotment. While sorry about the circumstances I take full advantage of his absence to plant the place up with crops I like: everlasting spinach again but also chard, lettuce and onions. I also decide to have another go at cabbage.

To cater for Dad's tastes, I sow Brussels sprouts in pots on the kitchen windowsill, plus runner beans to transfer to my bean tower later on. We should be on for a good crop of berries this year and the potatoes Dad left in from last year are, as hoped, sprouting anew.

It's with talk of this that I finally entice him down to the plot. He thoroughly enjoys the visit, being delighted with his burgeoning potato tops and making full use of the chance to check his shed and his fence.

He also takes a detour on the way out to visit the three sets of chickens who live in varying degrees of squalor on nearby plots. Influenced perhaps by hit films of yesteryear like *Dr Doolittle* and the *Horse Whisperer*, he crouches as best he can on the path by their respective coops and makes a noise like a creaking door.

I'm reminded of how much he loves animals. He had a Cocker Spaniel as a child, which meant that I too had a Cocker Spaniel as a child. Smudge, a slow portly animal, used to disappear from our back garden on warm afternoons and come back with whole joints of meat in his slobbering flews.

He never got much of a ticking-off. Dad admired his nerve and the fact he'd brought home the bacon (and lamb and chicken and once, a foil wrapped pack of cheese sandwiches.) The nearby Fantail Hotel had a Michelin starred restaurant and Dad thought it must have an open larder. That seemed unlikely. But then so did the idea of Smudge, a blunderbuss of a dog, doing anything stealthy or agile. We came close to roasting and eating the lamb and chicken ourselves (that's the sort of thing people did back in the 1970s) but Mum's caution prevailed and Smudge got to polish them off by himself.

When I left home, I got a dog of my own. Maxi and his successor Dog MS were both shepherd dogs. Dad has loved them as his own, spending hours playing with them in the garden or sitting fondling their heads while they stain his trouser leg with dribble.

'What a lovely dog he is,' he says about Dog MS, forgetting she's a girl. But slips like this don't bother her. She reciprocates his love in full. In fact, she throws herself at the feet of any man in a flat cap, thinking they are all Dad.

Dad has 'previous' with birds too. At their old kitchen window in the Cotswolds, he and Mum would take their elevenses watching sparrows, finches and tits of all kinds descend on his home-made feeders. He would see squirrels off with a home-made catapult.

So perhaps it's not surprising about his new friends.

Perhaps it's not surprising either that this visit seems to break his duck, and over the next couple of weeks he comes back several times, to check the progress of the potatoes ('they're shooting up!') and chat to the chickens.

Interestingly after a couple of visits, they start to talk back to him. At the sound of his footsteps, brown, black and white hens rush in a feathery tide to the fence, clucking and pecking at each other's eyes in their haste to get to the front. Their foreman the cockerel doesn't join in the melee but stands at a distance looking outraged and making sudden sharp little head movements with machine precision.

Even once Dad has moved on, the hens stay at the fence squawking. It makes you wonder what he has said to them. It makes him wonder, too. Let's hope they don't start flocking to the fence every time a man in a flat cap comes along. The cockerel will have to introduce a work-to-rule system, or egg-laying production will be seriously down this year.

Early June 2011. TV gardening

Early summer brings with it a slew of TV gardening programmes.

Before getting an allotment, my eyes skipped automatically across the listings for these programmes as though they weren't there. I knew who Alan Titchmarsh was because he was born in the next street to ours and sometimes comes to switch on the Christmas lights. And everyone's heard of Monty Don, the welly-wearing woman's crumpet and an eloquent speaker and writer about mental health. But as to what either of them did when they got down and dirty, I had no idea.

But one pleasant evening when Dad and Mr MS are washing up in the kitchen, I find myself still sitting on the settee twenty minutes into Gardener's World, the remote gone limp in my hand. Carol Klein's segment is on. I realise I am coming to admire her passion for her garden, her discernment in hiring interesting-looking men to finesse bush and hedge and her roping in of the camera-shy Mr CK for the heavy work.

I also love the scenes in her shed, where she is found in the middle of the night pricking out and potting seedlings and topping her pots off with a layer of grit, making beautiful gravelled oblongs like miniature Zen gardens. I have no idea why she does this but I know a pleasing ritual when I see one.

I realise that I mustn't get too carried away by TV gardening, of course. It's sheer fantasy to believe that our allotment will ever look like Monty Don's vegetable garden at Longmeadow, even when riddled with the black gold that is currently being cooked up under our Axminster-carpet-lidded compost heap.

If I want relevant gardening tips, I should probably consult one of the taciturn old gimmers down at the allotment. Nevertheless, I make a resolution to watch the whole series of Gardener's World. This is dangerous territory, I know. I'll soon be listening to Gardeners' Question Time on BBC Radio 4, a place from which few return.

Dad and Mr MS come in. Neither of them will have any truck with gardening programmes so I offer to change channel. 'I suppose we'd better sit through a bit of the news,' says Dad, gloomily. Mr MS watches the news with interest but it soon turns out there is nothing of relevance to Dad, in other words no footage of natural disasters nor any science news. 'Bloody politicians!' he says when Gordon Brown comes on. 'They're all the same.'

'Ordinary people trying to do a difficult job,' mutters Mr MS, who is a member of the Labour Party. 'Would you like a cup of tea, Ted?'

It's often difficult to find programmes Dad will enjoy when he is at our house. Unlike him, we don't have Sky TV. We tried an astronomy series but he has no time for the modern-day presentation style. 'Who's that idiot? Why's he drawing a diagram of the solar system in the sand with a stick then shouting over his shoulder while he runs up a hill? And why do we have to have all that bloody music?' Thank goodness for Ice Road Truckers, which for some reason, Dad loves, along with re-runs of Porridge and Rising Damp.

But he always brightens when the weather forecast comes on. 'Ah, a bit of weather, that's more like it. This is what people really want to know about,' he says now. Afterwards, he says he doesn't know why he watches it as they nearly always get it wrong and you might as well ignore everything they say. But he hangs onto their every word all the same, just as I am starting to hang onto the words of Carol Klein and Monty Don.

Dad may or may not go to the allotment tomorrow and he may or may not take his umbrella. I may or may not visit the garden centre to buy some grit. But we both appreciate the fleeting feeling of being in the know, no matter how illusory it turns out to be.

Late June 2011. Velveteen visitor

Towards the end of June, just when I most need to be down at the allotment, I'm forced to take a break. Hip bursitis strikes and walking is difficult, much less bending. Luckily, I manage to get a few seedlings in before it gets too bad: runner beans, cabbage, a pumpkin plant and a few outdoor tomatoes planted against the fence on the west facing side of plot. I'd already bobbed a few King Edwards in, in case Dad's Home Guards didn't come up. But in the event, all the spuds are flourishing, covering several beds with their dark green rosettes and making our plot look like a going concern.

Dad's spud and chicken checking visits have tailed off, though. He finally presented his spreadsheet at the local surgery and has now had a 24-hour heart monitor test and then one that lasted three days. These stopped him going about his normal business, even though the GP advised him to continue as normal.

'Yes, but I didn't quite like to,' he says. 'It didn't seem right.' And neither test showed anything wrong, much to his disgust.

'I'm afraid I had a bit of an up and downer with the surgery,' he admits one morning at his flat.

'Oh?' I say, pretending to chew on a stale Jacob's Orange Club biscuit while slipping bits into my handbag. Biscuit deceit is hereditary: in British Home Stores café Mum and Dad always took their own, breaking pieces off under the table and only swallowing when no-one was looking.

'That bloody woman is trying to put me on heart tablets,' says Dad. 'What good will that do? It's just a stab in the dark! I told her I'd had a pre-syncope and she had the nerve to ask me what I understood by the term. Then she said, "why don't you just describe exactly what symptoms you're experiencing?" As if I was a five year old!'

Dad hates being treated as anything less than a professional, even when it isn't his profession. This isn't good for his heart I think and say various reasonable things in a tone which strikes me as unfortunate. Dad pounds his fist suddenly on the table, sending coffee jumping out of our mugs. 'Whose side are you on?'

I stare at him in dismay. 'Yours, of course!' It isn't the right moment to ask him to help on the allotment. I walk home, worrying about Dad's heart and worrying too about the allotment going to rack and ruin in our absence. As soon as I'm through the door, I snap at Mr MS over a trifle then burst into tears. Mr MS makes me a cup of tea or 'boil' as we like to call it.

'I'll go down to the allotment, if you can tell me what needs doing,' he offers. It's sweet of him, but I know from previous experience that I can't let him go down there unsupervised. Over the past year, although he has appeared interested when I talk about crops, he has retained absolutely nothing I've told him and still can't tell the difference between parsley and grass.

'It's okay,' I say.

'Want one of these?' he asks, flourishing a packet of dark chocolate digestives. I wave them away. I've already had one third of an Orange Club Biscuit today that I didn't enjoy because it was stale. What a waste of calories! Mr MS, who rarely exercises and lives on biscuits and Full English Breakfasts, never puts on an ounce. I, who swim, do Pilates, walk the dog and play table tennis four times a week, have to constantly monitor my food intake.

I try to drink my boil but it is scalding hot. 'The jobs don't really matter,' I say, bitter. 'It's just that I miss going down there.' Suddenly I am close to tears again.

'Oh dear,' says Mr MS. 'Look, why don't you go down now? I'll put your boil in a flask. You could sit on the bench and just enjoy being there.' It's a reasonable enough suggestion, I suppose. But it makes me feel worse. 'Because I'll hate seeing all the work that needs doing and not being able to do it!' I cry. Mr MS stares. I don't know if that's because I'm shouting or because I'm expressing a viewpoint that is totally alien to him. 'Sorry,' I say. 'I'll give it a try.'

Limping to the plot, I see that while I've been idle, other creatures haven't. The place is covered in little mounds of soil, very finely churned as if a mini rotavator has been at work. My cry of alarm brings one of our allotment neighbours over, the one who always wears a leather cowboy hat.

He reassures me that although Mr Mole, an insectivore, scoots under the roots, he won't actually munch our lunch (those aren't his exact words, but that's what he means). So it's best to do nothing. I agree. The physio has already said that doing nothing must become my new forte, my new modus operandi (not her exact words either). The neighbour also lends me his hoe, suggesting that even if I can't bend to weed, I can lop the heads off the weeds growing around my crops.

It is very kind of him. I thank him then sit on the bench and drink my boil. I try to just listen to the bird song and the rustling of the leaves. I manage it for a few seconds. The sounds are enchanting and I can see a different version of myself, at another time, in another universe, sitting and idling away an hour in their company. It would be a kind of meditation. But here and now, I just can't do it. Lounging on the plot at the peak of summer! I can almost see the weeds growing. Stowing the hoe in the shed, I decide to go for a hobble around the other plots instead.

This proves to be, in Mr MS speak, a 'doubler' – something that kills two birds with one stone. I am getting gentle exercise (recommended) and gathering allotment intel at the same time. I discover that more new creatures have arrived a few plots down: three pigs. A notice on their gate says they've been brought in to clear the undergrowth. They seem to have done that already, including eating their own shed door.

By the time I get home, I'm in a far better mood. Then Mr MS says he'll ring Dad and arrange to take him out for a drive later in the week. 'A change of scene might help him get things back in perspective,' he says.

'Will you really?' I ask. Even thinking about their trip together makes me breathe more easily. Mr MS is a treasure.

Then Dad rings and it seems there has been progress on another front too. The GP has agreed to a 7-day heart monitor. Dad will be fitted with it in a few days' time.

'Well, that's good news,' I say, cheerily. Dad mutters something. 'While you're waiting for that to be sorted,' I add, 'you can go and see the chickens.'

'Maybe,' says Dad darkly. 'And maybe not.'

I realise I am cajoling him, even while trying not to. Unfortunately, it comes to me as naturally as breathing. I put the phone down and stare at my hands. I feel sorry for Dad, deprived of the chicken's company. More ridiculously I feel sorry for the chickens, deprived of him.

Suddenly a solution presents itself. I could take over from Dad as Chief Chicken Visitor until he is back up and running. I could include the pygmy goats on my rounds, and of course there are now the three little pigs. In other words, I'll do as Dad was doing before he was derailed by his health issues, or more accurately by his reaction to them. Armed with my hoe and my new attitude, I'll find a new way to enjoy the allotments.

I rejoice inwardly, especially when I remember from somewhere that pigs love courgettes and that I have some in the fridge that I'd been wondering how to use up. It's a doubler if ever there was one.

Early July 2011. Love among the lettuces

I spend a couple of weeks enjoying visiting our plot purely to say hello to the Lady of Shallot, lop the heads off one or two weeds then scoot around to see the animals on the other plots. But calling on the pigs one day I see that a tall dark stranger has arrived on the plot opposite them. He has broad shoulders, a manly chest and an unflinching gaze. He strikes me immediately as the strong silent type, seeing much and saying nowt.

He wears a faded denim shirt with pockets, suggesting practicality. He has proper shoes. Even more appealing, he is modest and plays down his obvious attractions: despite the impressive breadth of his chest, he keeps his sleeves rolled down and his shirt buttoned to the neck, even on a hot summer's day like today.

Alright, so he wears beige slacks. But his hands compensate for that. Instead of the usual lumpy gloves that pass for fingers around here he has – ladies and some gentlemen may want to sit down at this point – multicoloured windmills. Oh, how they whir in the stiff breeze! How they intimidate the birds! How they glitter as he looms threateningly over the broad beans, his hands full of rainbows!

I make discreet enquiries of the human digging the soil behind him and discover that his name is Harry. I hurry to our plot to tell the Lady of Shallot. She has already noticed him it seems, as she is beaming in his direction and occasionally rotating her head, like Linda Blair in The Exorcist.

He plays it cool, of course, staring fixedly, if thoughtfully, at the ground. As anyone knows who has dealt with a man like Harry, there is doubtless a torrent of emotion raging beneath his calm exterior. He may look uninterested but he is just treating 'em mean to keep 'em keen. Or perhaps, while tough in matters of scaring birds, he is shy when it comes to love and only dares sneak a look at her when her head is revolving the other way.

Things look very promising. I head home in high spirits, delighted on the Lady's behalf. But within a few days, it all goes horribly wrong. You will be wondering how. Surely, you will assume, a man like Harry recognises an allotment as a long-term commitment? Surely a man with such spectacular appendages can't be a fly-by-night? You're right on both counts. Harry stays, keeping his stolid, vaguely menacing vigil. And the Lady of Shallot still grins and spins. But the course of true love never did run smooth.

Passing Harry's plot a few days later, I fancy that his gaze is more downcast than before. He looks a little heartbroken, even. And then I see why. Our immediate neighbour has erected a massive polytunnel between his plot and our plot. I rush over to the Lady. She is still looking over at Harry, trying to catch his eye. But all she can see now is his vague shape through cloudy plastic.

I sink onto the bench. This is a major setback. Although in theory she could move to the front of our plot, where she could see him around the edge of the polytunnel, there are no crops there to protect, and a Lady has her pride. I speak, not from experience (alas) but from the vast numbers of self-help books I read before I met Mr MS. I suspect the Lady is made of stronger stuff than I, though. I search her face for clues. She doesn't give much away. I reckon she's decided to leave it up to Harry to make the next move. She could be waiting a long time.

Late July 2011. Three little pigs

As July wears on, Mr MS also begins visiting the allotments regularly, not to help on the plot or anything, but to watch the pigs grow fatter by the second.

One morning he watches them shove each other out of the way to get at a handful of swede peelings. 'They'll eat anything,' he says admiringly. Then he presents them with some Tesco's mushrooms that have gone slimy in the fridge – and discovers they won't. He settles for scratching their bristly heads through the gate. He doesn't mind their stinking to high heaven, being plastered in mud and pestered by ceaseless fleas. That doesn't put other visitors off either. Children swarm down the river path to poke pea pods through the fence.

Late July brings a definite diagnosis for Dad – heart failure. He is alarmed, but reassured by a cardiology consultant he judges to be 'the right age, not too young but not too old to be past it' that a pacemaker can be fitted and will make all the difference.

It sounds promising but I find it impossible not to worry about him. As a distraction the day before his op, I go to visit the pigs. But on their plot, I can find no sign of their itchy pink bodies. I peer around the place, trying to see inside their doorless shed, refusing to believe the obvious.

But they are gone and that can mean only one thing. I walk slowly to our plot and chuck the now redundant pea pods onto the compost heap. I imagine the visiting children's disappointment and the pathetic age-appropriate explanations given by accompanying adults.

As for me, I am not good with Death despite years of meditation. I am soppy even about weak seedlings. Chuck 'em out, says every gardening guru under the sun. But I prefer to waste valuable time and windowsill space trying to nurture the half dead back to life. Perhaps it's the mothering instinct gone rogue. I should have had children. Then again, there must be thousands of childless women in the world who aren't watering spindly Brussels Sprouts seedlings out of a specially made bottle every morning. My saviour complex explains my adoption of the neurotic Dog MS, a stray in an earlier life. On my choice of the men in my life (before Mr MS, naturally), I remain silent.

But back to the pigs and when I burst through the back door wailing, Mr MS is at the cooker making a bacon sandwich. 'Oh well,' he says, on hearing my sorry tale, 'We've all got to go sometime.'

I shoot him a look. 'I mean the pigs, not your Dad,' he says quickly. I forgive any insensitivity. I know he views the op as routine and unlike me isn't one to dwell on all the things that might go wrong.

We spend the evening with Dad. I am subdued and Dad, sombre, rejects all Mr MS's attempts at humour. 'It's a serious thing, this operation, you know,' he snaps. He doesn't muster a smile all night, even through three Rising Damp reruns.

It is good to find him calm the following morning when we pick him up at 6am. He comments on the fields and the dry-stone walls that go by outside the car window. The near ones pass quickly, the distant ones slowly, as if we're travelling on the rim of a giant wheel.

When we arrive at the small hospital, Dad insists on going in alone. I watch him cross the car park in his old padded anorak and tweed cap, carrying his overnight bag. As he's swallowed by the big glass double doors I remember how, when I was a student going back up North after Christmas, he used to drive me to Kings Cross and watch me all the way on to the train.

Mr MS squeezes my shoulder. 'He'll be fine, don't you worry.'

'Yes, but you never DO worry, do you?' I snap.

It is nasty, and on the way home I apologize and say I'll make bangers, mash and beans for tea. Later, there's a welcome phone call saying that the operation has been a success and the following morning when Mr MS is at work, I drive over to the hospital in the camper van to pick Dad up. It is a lovely sunny morning.

He is in his room preparing to leave. 'Hello love!' he says, relief written all over his face.

'How do you feel?' I ask him.

'Right as rain,' he says.

On the way off the ward, he thanks everyone profusely and chooses the stairs over the lift to go down to the ground floor. He doesn't even let me carry his overnight bag. On the drive back in the camper van, he regales me with a description of his operation in tremendous detail, which he was allowed to watch on a screen above the operating table.

'The only thing I don't like,' he says, 'is the fact that the pacemaker is battery operated. I mean, what if the battery's a dud, like the one that garage once sold me?'

It's a fair point, but luckily he doesn't dwell on it. He goes back to the gory details of the op again. I'm grateful for the rattle and creak of the camper van, which drown at least some of his account out. I hope I can get him home before I pass out at the wheel.

August 2011. Halfwits

Over the next couple of weeks, it is wonderful to go back to normal. Dad has no further pre-syncopes, or any whatever-he-understands-by-the-terms either.

The topic of the op still dominates our conversations, though. 'How about a visit to the plot later?' I say as he pauses for breath one morning. It's August and the leaves on the treetops outside his first-floor window are scattered with yellows and reds.

'Maybe,' he says, 'in a few days' time.' He pours the coffee. 'The thing is, I reckon that chap did a pretty decent job. Do you know, I asked him if at 88 I was his oldest patient. Guess what he said?'

I sigh inwardly. 'What?'

'He said last week he'd installed a pacemaker in a man of 98! That takes a bit of skill, doesn't it?'

'Yes, it must do,' I say.

He passes me an Orange Club. Something strange has happened to the wrapper: it looks greasy.

'When did you buy these biscuits, Dad?' I ask.

'Oh, I forget. Some time ago,' he says, unwrapping his. Its chocolate covering has white tidemarks. He takes a bite anyway.

'If it had been left to that bloody woman at the Health Clinic,' he says, mouth full, 'I'd be dead by now. Trying to fob me off with tablets! I'm thinking of putting in a complaint about her to the surgery.'

I sigh out loud this time. 'Really?'

'It's about time somebody did.' He screws his biscuit wrapper up and lobs it hard into the waste paper basket.

If Mr MS was here, he would pretend to agree with Dad. It is what he generally does, a) for the sake of a quiet life and b) because Dad won't listen to him if he disagrees. If I go along with Dad too much though, I feel as if I'm perjuring my soul.

'Do you really want to do that, Dad?' I ask now. 'It'll be a load of hassle and you probably won't get anywhere.' What I really mean is: you've been given a new lease of life. Why not try to enjoy it?

'Maybe,' he says. 'Maybe not. You see, what those doctors really want is to kill all us old folks off. Get us off their books.'

Having friends who are GPs, I am annoyed on their behalf and decide it's best not to reply. I sip my coffee and try to switch off a bit as he chunters on. He mentions medical negligence and the General Medical Council. It sounds as if he has already done some research on his computer. I see long months of barbed letters and furious phone calls ahead and there's nothing I can do to stop it. As I sit there trying not to listen, it strikes me that having barneys with people he regards as halfwits is at the very heart and soul of the man. Then he surprises me.

'Oh well,' he says in a different tone. 'I don't suppose any of it matters very much.'

I'm struck by the sadness in his voice. But I know he's finally giving me permission to change the subject; permission almost, to cheer him up. I waste no time.

'No, I don't suppose it does,' I say. 'And anyway, we should be able to dig up some of your Home Guard spuds soon, from last year.'

'Really?' he says. 'Do you think they'll be ready?'

'Yes,' I say. 'I furtled for them yesterday.'

'You did what?'

'Furtled. Dug my hand down near one of the plants and felt around.' I remember the white-haired old chap at the allotment who instructed me and his smirk when I glanced at my fingernails, suddenly split and grimy with Yorkshire clay, which would prove nigh on impossible to completely remove. It was worth it, though, to feel the cool hard subterranean forms of the potatoes.

'I've never heard of furtling,' says Dad.

'Me neither. But it's going to be a good crop.'

'I knew it was a good idea to leave those taters in,' he says. He flourishes an imaginary cigar, takes a puff on it then taps imaginary ash onto the ground. I laugh. It is a gesture I've seen a million times before. But I'm very pleased to see it now.

Early September 2011. Big veg

Over the next few days, I dig out plenty of big healthy spuds while Dad supervises from the bench.

'No, no, no, you're going at it all wrong! Dig further away from the plant or you'll put the fork through them,' he shouts. I grit my teeth. His pacemaker seems to be giving a new lease of impatience as well as a new lease of life. But I'm happy he's out and about and also happy that my hip bursitis has largely gone, even though little 'itises' are following the big one like pilot fish in a whale's wake.

I unearth an enormous spud, which will weigh in later at 2lbs. Dad, who has decided to wear 2 pairs of £1 reading specs one on top of the other rather than forking out £300 at the opticians, can hardly believe the evidence of his six eyes. 'Now that's a potato among potatoes,' he says. 'It'll keep me going for a month.'

And the spuds aren't the only oversized triumphs at the allotments. This second year is proving more fruitful than the first, for all us newbies. One couple, who have been on holiday, come back to find their cabbages big enough to appear on road maps.

I imagined that having an allotment would make us immune from vegetable gifts. But I notice that innocent observations like 'cracking courgettes!' or 'beautiful beans!' bring hope to other allotmenteers' eyes. 'Please take a few,' they plead. It is an unfeeling person who looks into those desperate faces and says 'no'. And so it is with the cabbage couple. I take delivery of a huge head of Savoy. There is method in my madness: I'm about to go away for a few days with work.

Before that though I have to carry the cabbage to the car. I struggle with its weight and bulk. Perhaps it is already developing its own gravity system.

Mr MS and I have a spacious kitchen. But the arrival of the gargantuan green makes it look small. The legs of the kitchen table tremble and Mr MS backs away across the kitchen saying 'no, no, no.'

I ignore this. 'I know how much you like cabbage,' I say cruelly. 'And as you know, I'm away from tomorrow. So this is your project.' Luckily one of Mr MS's friends is coming to stay in my absence. He's a vegetarian, which may help.

I leave for Northampton and phone home a few days later. Mr MS and I manage to talk pleasantly for a while, but we both know where the conversation is headed. 'The thing is, we haven't made much of an impact on the Savoy yet,' he says. I tut and am about to launch into a ticking off when a memory from primary school surfaces.

I am sitting over a bowl of tapioca in the school canteen. My friends have gone back to the playground. Under Miss Boorman's hard gaze I put a large spoonful of the foul spawn into my mouth, where it goes round and round. I try to swallow. But there is a volcanic eruption from within. My head jerks forwards and the tapioca descends in a vile stinging stream from my nose.

'Don't worry about it,' I say to Mr MS now. 'It's awful being made to eat something you dislike.'

Having readied himself for a bollocking, he is astonished. 'What? I didn't say I didn't like it. Listen, we'll try and break through the outer atmosphere tonight, I promise.'

When I return home, he swears they have eaten ten leaves. But the cabbage looks undiminished. Perhaps it is evolving, learning how to replenish itself from thin air. I ring Dad. 'Remember that website you found with all those turnip recipes?' I say. 'Mr Neep?'

'Did I?' he says. 'Well, if you say so.'

'Well, now we need Mrs Brassica.'

'Now that's something I can do. Leave it with me, love,' he says. Later that evening he rings back. 'Good news! I've found a site with 200 recipes all involving cabbage.'

'Great,' I say. 'We may have to try them all.'

Late September 2011. Bringing in the harvest

The gift of the massive Savoy is now safely behind us. We ate most of it mixed with mash and sprinkled with grated Cheddar then baked, a simple but satisfying recipe from the website Dad found. During that fortnight, it was terrifically windy.

It was tempestuous outdoors too and at the allotments only the crops that kept their heads down survived. Apples and plums plummeted and there were downpours of damsons, like purple rain. Brassicas were battered and sunflowers summarily beheaded by the wind's guillotine. On our plot, we picked some runner beans before the wind blew my tower down and then picked the rest at ground level.

Now it is only the low riders of the fruit and veg world that remain unscathed: blackberries, potatoes, cabbages, the tomatoes that were miraculously sheltered by the fence and the pumpkin. Actually, I can't image anything defeating the pumpkin. The stealthy, rapid way it has covered the ground all summer has been terrifying. If you sit still and watch you can almost see it grow. It seems to be heading for the A65 to Leeds.

So there is some harvesting to do. Dad has asked to be excused, not just on health grounds but because he's not really 'a cabbage man.' 'Not much of a pumpkin man either,' he adds. Furthermore, he is spotted buying potatoes from Tommy Tesco. He ate a lot of Home Guard spuds but doesn't like my King Edwards. 'I like a nice boiled spud,' he says. 'Yours go abroad in the pan.'

Then Dog MS begs off too. There are some urgent sticks in her 'in' tray and some long overdue barking to do, especially at the ironing board, which needs taking down a peg or two.

As Harvest Manager, it's obviously not my role to do the grunt work of bending, picking and lugging heavy veg about. So it gets passed down the chain to Mr Mandy Sutter. After making protracted notes in his diary, a prelude vital to the success of any mission, he makes it to the plot, where he loads cabbages into carrier bags and unearths spuds of pink and golden hue. I pick a few berries and say I need to be careful not to give myself another bursitis.

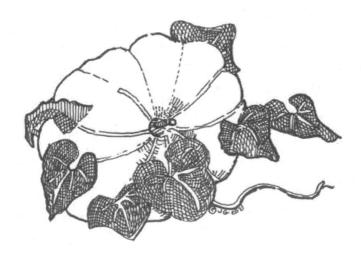

We pile them into our new wheelbarrow and head back to our camper van. On the way there, Mr MS slows to a standstill. He has spotted a whole hammock full of onions on a neighbour's plot. They lounge, enjoying an afternoon of autumn sunshine. He eyes them enviously.

I crack a whip across his glistening flanks. He doesn't budge. But I have a secret card up my sleeve. 'I'm thinking of making a blackberry and apple loaf when we get home,' I say casually. 'And I think there's some cream left to go on it.'

His eyes flare and he moves off with his load towards our camper van. I am triumphant: the harvest is in.

Early October 2011. A right pickle

Our substantial harvest brings tasks in its wake. We have to figure out what to do with all the produce. The blackberries and potatoes are easy. The berries go straight in the freezer; the spuds are wiped clean then layered between sheets of newspaper in a sack that goes into a cubby hole at the top of the cellar steps. The two pumpkins go atop a kitchen cabinet. The tomatoes and cabbage, however, will take a bit more work.

Unfortunately, Dad, Mr MS, Dog MS and I are all pickle averse. Mr MS had a piccalilli 'incident' aged 17 and hasn't touched the stuff since. Dog MS tried to eat a pickled onion and had a sneezing fit that nearly took her head off. Dad is a mono-condimentalist and that condiment is HP sauce. And I've not been keen since someone put some Branston pickle down the toilet as a 'joke'.

But now that we're allotmenteers, we must change. The idea that fresh vegetables only last a week must be scotched. What can't be endured must be cured.

It has been a bad year for blight (or a good one, if you are a blighter) and the tomatoes went straight from green to rotten, leaving out that useful bit in between. They hung, brown and bulbous, looking disturbingly like diseased nuts (yes, I do mean those sorts of nuts.)

But we did rescue some of the green ones before they succumbed. I find a recipe for chutney and chop them up, lobbing in some red and yellow ones from the greengrocer too. They roil in the pan together like traffic light stew. A shame it all has to turn brown in the end.

We sample it before leaving it to mature and despite being the same colour as the blighted tomatoes, it tastes cracking. I use it to top a Bath Oliver and some cave aged Emmental. Mr MS, who finds these ingredients pretentious, substitutes with a Jacob's cream cracker and a Dairylea triangle.

Pickling doesn't end there. A friend, hearing about our cabbage crop, lends me a fermenting pot. Ideal, he says, for making sauerkraut. Mr MS is suspicious. 'Yes, but what IS sauerkraut, exactly? Do you eat it hot or cold? And what with?'

'It's pickled cabbage,' I say. 'You can eat it any way you want.' I don't know why I always pretend to know everything when talking to Mr MS. I've no idea whether you can eat it hot. But I begin reeling off different kinds of German sausage, unmoved by his baffled expression. Then I relent. 'Hot dogs,' I say.

Suddenly he is a different man. 'Hot dogs? Why didn't you say so before?'

That's the thing with menfolk. Eventually you have to speak their language.

To be accurate, sauerkraut doesn't involve pickling, but fermenting. Or so I discover watching the exceptionally long DVD that comes with the pot, where a German chap with massive sideburns and adjoining handlebar moustache holds forth about the health benefits of fermented foods. It is only after an hour of exposition that he finally begins explaining how to make the actual sauerkraut. For him it obviously isn't just about passing on a recipe. It's a religion.

That's the thing about allotmenteering. You don't have to look very far into any of its aspects before you stumble across arcane sub-cultures peopled with evangelical folk with excess facial hair and home knitted trousers (or no trousers at all in the case of World Naked Gardening Day). There are feature film-length DVDs and books about recycling your own piss, there are Potato Days, there are Scarecrow Festivals – the list goes on.

But back to the sauerkraut and eventually, after a hell of a lot of shredding, salting and pressing everything down into the pot, where it makes its own juice, it's ready to leave for a few weeks. I put it on the cellar steps, where it should keep nice and cool.

I plan to lift the lid on it next month. If I can get the vision of the handlebar moustache out of my mind, I may even eat some.

Mid-October 2011. Top Plot

I have always loved autumn but I love it more than ever in this second year of allotmenteering. I live with the promise of a long brutal winter to come that freezes the ground and makes digging impossible. But in October, Dad rings with strange news. 'You'll never guess what! We've been awarded a prize!'

'A prize? Who by?' I ask.

'Oh, I don't know. Some idiot or other. But who cares? The point is we've won Best Allotment!'

'What?' I say, wondering if he has got hold of the wrong end of some sort of stick. It seems so unlikely. But he goes on, giving a convincing level of detail. 'We're invited to a presentation tea this Saturday. We can wedge up on cucumber sarnies and cream scones!'

The tea is being held at a local posherie. 'Really?' I say. 'I can't believe it.'

Other plot holders have raised far better crops than us this year. I suppose our allotment is laid out more prettily than some, with its central grass ring enclosing fruit bushes, but that's the only thing to distinguish it. I decide it must be a mercy prize.

'Oh well. That'll be lovely,' I say, belatedly. I put the phone down. 'Tea out with Dad,' I say to Dog MS. 'God help me.'

For Dad retains a schoolboy scorn for 'occasions,' or indeed any event where one is expected to behave politely. He finds it all ridiculous and after a few red wines, he has been known to jeer from the back. Once when Mr MS and I took him to a local jazz event, he waited for a quiet bit then shouted, 'this isn't jazz! This is a bloody racket!' There won't be music at the prize giving but I imagine there will be plenty of other things to object to, including speeches, which he loathes.

He has also recently jettisoned his £2,000 hearing aid because the batteries are too expensive (5p each) and taken to shouting 'Eh?' when he can't hear. He seems to have given up on his teeth completely, home-made ones or otherwise.

He is therefore no oil painting. This would matter less if he refrained from commenting unkindly on other people's weight, height, nose, ears, teeth or lack of them and hair or lack of it in the exceptionally loud voice common to those who refuse to wear hearing aids.

I wish, disloyally, that I could take a different family member to the tea, one who has excelled at digging this year and eaten all the produce no-one else wanted like windfall apples, wormy potatoes and stringy runner beans. But the invitation says dogs aren't allowed.

I ring the organizers and ask if we can bring an extra human. 'If that fails, I'll come,' says Mr MS. But the organisers say no. 'Never mind,' says Mr MS too quickly, pleased that his Saturday afternoon session in front of Match of the Day remains unthreatened. 'He's your Dad! Take him. It'll be a lovely trip out.'

I remember our last lovely trip out. We went to the garden centre soon after Dad's pacemaker was fitted. I thought a bit of gentle trolley pushing would be good exercise. But Dad himself was anything but gentle. When the woman in front of him hesitated in the pansy aisle, he drove his trolley hard into hers, muttering, 'Giddon out of it.' She gave a startled cry and dropped her handbag. He, of course, pretended it was an accident.

'He gets quite lairy these days,' I say.

'I'm sorry,' says Mr MS, 'but if you think your Dad qualifies as lairy, you've led a sheltered life.'

'Alright,' I say quickly, before he can start talking about his drinking buddies back in the day. 'Point taken.' He is right: I am being uncharitable. I resolve to worry less what other people think and enjoy an afternoon out with my Dad.

And in the event, none of the things I worried about happen. Dad keeps his thoughts about other people's appearance to himself. He can't actually hear the speeches, so talks over them, but it doesn't matter because the speakers have microphones and he doesn't. He keeps saying loudly that tea is all very well but where is the real drink? But even a wuss like me can cope with that. He is presented with a silvery plaque and will be its custodian for a year. 'Cheap-looking thing, isn't it?' he says loudly while I wonder whether, having won the prize and tasted the high life, I'll now be driven to try and win it every year.

But as we leave the hotel, something happens that I'm not expecting. Dad loses his footing and falls down two stone steps to land flat on his face at the bottom. Time stands still and for several seconds I can't move to help him, like in a nightmare. Then I rush forwards, anticipating at least a dozen broken bones. But, 'I'm alright,' he says again and again. 'I'm alright.'

His face is puce. Getting him back onto his feet takes enormous effort on both our parts. We limp to a nearby bench and sit. Strangely, from the moment he falls to the moment we finally get up to leave, which must be half an hour, no-one emerges from the hotel or passes by on the pavement. The whole incident goes oddly unwitnessed. He doesn't want doctors involved so when his face is a better colour, I drive him home.

I don't sleep a wink all night and ring as soon as decently possible in the morning.

'Me? I'm right as rain, love,' he says cheerily. 'Oh, apart from a small round bruise on my right thigh.'

'Oh?' My mind spins wildly in search of an explanation. Could that be the sign of a stroke? An embolism?

'Probably caused by the pound coin in my trouser pocket,' he says.

I breathe out. His lack of broken bones, wounds or serious bruises is even more miraculous than us winning the Best Allotment prize.

The following week, we hear that the hotel is going bust. Perhaps it was sued by someone who fell down its (unmarked) stone steps.

November 2011. Love among the lettuces part II

Earlier in the year, you may remember that a romance at the allotments suffered a setback. The blossoming affair between Harry and the Lady of Shallot was stymied by an unfortunate erection. A polytunnel, appearing on the plot next door to ours, broke the all-important sight line between them.

Since then, the Lady has stuck firmly to her decision not to move. Being an old-fashioned girl (1833), she has decided it's up to rainbow-fingered Harry to make the next move. Mr MS, who seems to know how Harry's mind works, has advised me not to hold my breath. Incurable romantic that I am though, I find it hard to stop hoping. But the allotments get another blast of gale force winds and when I pop down to plant some overwintering broad beans and garlic, I see something that tests my optimism to the full.

Harry is stationed on a corner. Dog MS and I always pass him on the way to our plot. For months I have searched his face for clues as to how things stand between him and the Lady. In vain, because as noted before, Harry is master of the poker face. Even so, when as usual I try to catch his eye in passing, I'm shocked to see that he has taken his stubborn unresponsiveness to a new level. His face is now completely missing. I peer into his plot, wondering if he is merely saving face and it is hidden nearby, safe and sound. But it is nowhere to be seen. He has obviously become so afraid of losing face that he has, well, lost his face.

My fears are all for the Lady and how she might be feeling, assuming she's able to see what's happened through the murky plastic of the polytunnel. I hurry to our plot, nearly going arse over tit on the path, turned to mud by the rain.

If the state of affairs on Harry's plot made me blink, the Lady's plight makes me gasp aloud. She has seen only too well. She waited so patiently for things to improve but now the twists and turns of this fated love affair have taken their toll. She has lost her head.

It lies a little distance from her body, grinning up at the merciless grey sky. With another shock, I see that she has splintered at the waist. It is no exaggeration to describe her as a broken woman. It is hard to know what to do, so I run around lamenting.

Dog MS, keen to contribute, starts chewing the Lady's head. I shoo her away and give her a turnip to chew on instead. I crouch down by the Lady. She has taken off her Bacofoil ring, symbol of Harry's devotion, and thrown it onto the compost heap. Who can blame her?

Words are inadequate in the face of such disappointment. Clichés are all I can summon. 'He couldn't face real life', 'Don't worry, when one (shed) door closes, another opens' and 'you'll come out of this better and stronger! I'll find a thicker broom stick for your body.'

Cold comfort when one's heart is broken, I know. But I carry her head tenderly into the shed and lodge it on one of Dad's little triangular corner shelves. At least she is back in her bower. And at least she still has eyes and can see out of the window. I retrieve the Bacofoil ring. It is rather tinny. Vulgar, my

Mum would have called it. But I decide that we'll keep it, and pop it onto the shelf next to her head. Who knows, it may yet be called for. This romance may yet get its legs back, even if it is only one leg each.

December 2011. Of gnomes and names

Although I've been looking forward to the cold weather and the excuse not to visit the plot, now the winter is upon us with its indecently short days, I keep finding little jobs to do down there. The place must have more of a hold on me than I realise. Perhaps it's something to do with my new campingaz stove plus whistling kettle, mug and teabags. I never was one to visit the allotment, or indeed anywhere, without a Thermos full of 'boil' but I find that brewing up in the shed beats the flask system hands down.

It isn't just the taste of the tea. It's the walk to the tap and the joy of finding that the Council haven't yet turned the water off for winter. It's the delight when damp matches finally flare against damp box.

Once the kettle's on, it's the frequent breaks from whatever I'm doing to peer at the blue flame and rejoice that the gas hasn't run out. The whole process is so fragile that when the boil finally arrives, it's a miracle. A worthy substitute for seeing things grow.

And the lack of that growth is itself, paradoxically, motivating. Because if crops aren't growing then neither are weeds. So a cleared, dug-over bed stays cleared and dug over, a nice plain chocolate brown un-bespattered by Mother Nature's green paint pot.

The third boon is the post-gardening bath. There's simply no ablution to top it, especially in winter. Aching limbs are caressed by silken oiled water, grime floats out from under filthy fingernails, nettle stings are brutally revived to tingle afresh. The spent gardener lies contentedly under bubble bath foam as a landscape lies beneath clouds.

And then of course there's that special motivation that comes from members of one's family. When I tell Dad I'm still visiting the plot regularly, he says, 'can't think why. There must be bugger all to do down there at this time of year.'

As for Mr MS, when he 'pops down' to find me digging a bed over, something that I claimed only last month was unnecessary in winter, he stares at me with a look of distaste and says, 'crikey, don't overdo it. Sorry I can't stay. I've just come to get the loppers.' It seems one of our neighbours needs help tidying her bush. Later I hear that while lopping off twigs, he also lopped the head off her garden gnome.

But I'm getting side-tracked. I'm not the only allotmenteer who likes being there in winter and before he leaves with the loppers, Mr MS strikes up a conversation with our cowboy-hatted neighbour. Being something of a blurter, he lets slip that Dad and I call him The Farmer. 'Funny that,' says our neighbour, 'considering I'm a car mechanic.'

Things have the potential to turn frosty. But they don't: the Farmer (as I shall persist in calling him) admits that he calls another neighbour, who we know only by the disappointing title of Ian, 'Mr Windy.' Mr MS looks at me. The Farmer goes on. 'He put his shed up in a force ten gale, y'see.'

Mr MS titters obligingly but I can see he's disappointed by the explanation. He goes off muttering something that sounds like 'cock and balls.'

Later he claims it was 'coke and bowls', a mnemonic to help him remember a) to take some soft drink round to Dad's tonight to stop his glass being continually topped up with alcohol and b) to ask Dad whether he'd consider going to the local bowls club. A likely story. But I give him the benefit of the doubt. After all, it's only a matter of time before the decapitated gnome's mates come calling.

December 2011. Christmas lunch

Christmas Day comes round again. When Mum and Dad first moved up here, Mr MS and I formed a routine of cooking a bird at our house and taking it round to their flat to meet up with the sprouts and potatoes. It meant getting up early to put the turkey in because Dad had always eaten at midday and wasn't about to stop now. But since Mum died, we've had Dad round to our house for Christmas lunch and have managed to delay lunch in increments. This year it stands at 1pm, which gives us an hour's lie in compared to the old days. Even so, it doesn't feel enough.

Mr MS picks Dad up at eleven-thirty. He comes complete with a Tesco's carrier bag full of clanking bottles. First out of the bag is a Tesco's orange juice bottle containing a litre of decanted sherry (Dad buys sherry in quantity) and second comes a bottle of Moet.

'Oh, that's lovely, Dad,' I say. I'm not keen on sherry but champers always gets my vote.

I fear a third bottle but the other item in the bag is a hefty three-foot-long adjustable spanner.

'Thought that might be useful for getting the cork out,' says Dad. 'It'll double as a nut cracker.'

The saying 'using a sledgehammer to crack a nut,' comes to mind but I decide not to risk getting off on the wrong foot so early in the day.

Dad sits down at the kitchen table. 'Right, we'll get stuck in, shall we?' he says, unscrewing the cap on the sherry. 'We should see this off by lunchtime.'

I make my calculations: 90 minutes to drink 33cl of sherry each at 18% proof on an empty stomach. Twenty or even ten years ago I might have entertained this but the menopause seems to have put paid to my drinking days.

And Mr MS always was a lightweight, barely able to swallow down one whisky and coke before toppling over.

We brace ourselves. It is pointless saying no because if you do, Dad tops your glass up when you're not looking, in the cheery firm belief that you will be secretly grateful.

Being in our own home puts us at an advantage though and we're able to implement a strategy of gentle sipping and wafting into another room where we can pour the contents of our glasses into the equivalent of the aspidistra. We pull our crackers and put on our Christmas hats.

An hour of steady drinking doesn't improve Dad's mood. As the attentive reader will remember, he despises 'occasions' of any kind, even family ones. They seem to put him under a pressure that he finds intolerable. He has always hated Christmas, even before Mum died. Back in the day he would refuse to buy presents for Mum and me, then get so embarrassed when we gave him his that he'd rush out on Boxing Day and buy the first thing he could get hold of. One year there was only a garage open and he bought me an emergency windscreen repair kit. These days he solves it with a large box of Belgian chocolate seashells will a token square cut from last year's Christmas wrapping paper sellotaped onto the front. It is an improvement, and much appreciated.

Today he offers to help prepare the veg. He doesn't like roast potatoes so I always do some boiled ones for him. I give him some Maris Pipers to peel, sadly not from the allotment, though the roasted King Edwards that Mr MS and I will enjoy were dug only yesterday. We will all, however, be eating the meagre handful of Brussels Sprouts I picked. These blew open like buggered miniature cabbages on the central stalk, and now I've taken the shredded outer leaves off, they are tiny indeed. But they are home grown and that's what counts.

Dad, sitting at the kitchen table with his red paper crown akimbo, explodes suddenly. 'I can't do this job with a bloody knife!' Mr MS pulls a face at me and slips quietly into the sitting room. 'Where's that peeler?' Dad goes on. 'You know, the one Mum and I gave you in 1974?' He doesn't actually say 1974. But he has an astounding memory for everything Mum and he ever gave me.

126

I freeze for a moment before I remember that I do still have the peeler in the kitchen drawer and have had it there for years. I present it to him proudly. He straightens his crown. Unfortunately though, as he tackles the first Maris Piper, there is more cause for complaint. 'This peeler is completely blunt!'

'Oh?' I say.

'What have you done to it?' he barks.

'Well, nothing Dad,' I say in a reasonable voice. 'To be honest I hardly ever use it. I prefer...'

'You must have abused it in some way.'

I can see Mr MS in the sitting room, creasing up at the thought of peeler abuse.

But I'm nettled. I've never used the blinking thing, not even once. I always use knives. OK, so sometimes I might lop a finger tip off. Get over it.

'Look, I'll do it,' I say, glancing at the clock. The bird has already been resting for thirty minutes and I've got all my veg co-ordinated.

But Dad won't give up either the knife or the peeler now and proceeds at a snail's pace, alternating between one and the other. It's 12.52 before I can get hold of the spuds to cut them up small and get them in the pan. I put the sprouts on at the same time. They will probably be too hard. But never mind. Christmas dinner will be served up at 1pm sharp. Any slippage represents vital minutes I could have stayed in bed this morning, drinking my coffee and enjoying the sight of Dog MS getting high on excess dog chews.

I get the champagne out of the fridge and put it on the kitchen table. 'How about opening this, Dad?' I say.

'Now you're talking!' says Dad, and gets the gargantuan spanner out. His face has brightened considerably. I sigh inwardly but after a few moments of clattering pans around unnecessarily loudly, find myself giving up on my timings, otherwise known as 'if you can't beat 'em, join 'em.' I knock back the remains of my sherry, arrange the plates on the work surface and prepare to get plastered on champagne, menopause or not.

January 2012. Favourites

A bleak and cold January is upon us. It is an unrewarding month for even the most determined allotmenteer. Dad and Mr MS stay inside as much as possible and the only thing I can think of to do on the plot is tidy the shed while Dog MS guards the back fence, bristling when other dogs go past. In theory I could plant sweet peas in pots at this time of year but even I think that's taking gardening too far.

It's a good time of year for ordering seeds though, as all seed companies know. Dad has collected several catalogues and I find them stacked on his coffee table when I finish up at the plot and go round for a cup of tea and a warm up.

He has reached an age where letters are few and far between and he is grateful for anything that lands on his doormat. But before we get to the seed catalogues, there is another kind of missive to navigate – a brightly coloured printed letter with lots of capital letters telling him that he has won a diamond pendant and all he needs to do is claim it.

'I think I might send off for this,' he says, jabbing his finger on it. I see that he has already filled in the address box.

'Is that a good idea?' I ask.

'Well, it must be legit,' he says. 'They've got my name and address.' He hands me the magnifying class he has been using to peer at it. 'Have a look while I go and make the tea.'

I don't really need to look. 'What would you do with the pendant?' I ask as he comes back in with the two mugs teetering on his plywood tray.

'I thought you might like it.'

I glance at the cheap looking item on its silvery chain. 'That's a nice thought, Dad,' I say, a mixture of feelings roiling in my breast. Uppermost is anger at companies that target the vulnerable like this. 'Have you checked how much P&P you're signing up for?'

Dad sits down. 'What? Well, no, but it can't be much for a little thing like that, can it?'

It turns out to be £14.99. But Dad still isn't convinced that it's a scam. Filling the address box out in his increasingly tiny writing must have taken a while and it has hooked him in.

'Will you post it off for me love?' he asks, 'if I fetch you a stamp?'

I consider trying to change his mind, then recognise that this is one of those things I probably have to let go. He seems very chuffed about his free gift, which fact in itself might be worth £14.99.

'Of course,' I say. While Dad painstakingly makes out a cheque for the amount, I pick up one of the seed catalogues and begin leafing through. I find bright colours again, this time on flowers and vegetables, airbrushed and tinted to perfection. This is almost as much of a scam as the diamond pendant. The only difference is that when it comes to vegetables, I am willing to be seduced.

'What veg do you want to plant next year, Dad?' I ask, hoping he'll allow a change of subject.

I am in luck. 'Well, spuds,' he says, folding the coupon and cheque together into an envelope and licking the flap. 'Little beauties! Bung 'em in the ground, do nothing, dig 'em up a few months later.'

In Dad's view, vegetable crops are all either 'little beauties' or 'bloody washouts' and all spuds are little beauties. Except that is for some Christmas potatoes he bunged in last August. They grew nice green tops but produced nothing edible underground. They were bloody washouts.

'Any thoughts on varieties?' I ask.

'Well those Home Guard were superb, weren't they?' I nod and draw a red ring around the relevant seed potatoes in the catalogue.

'You're not actually buying them from that catalogue, are you?' he asks, anxious. 'Have you seen their prices? Bloody rip-off.'

'Oh, don't worry,' I say. 'It's just a visual record. So, what's next?'

Dad takes the wrapper off his Orange Club and wraps it carefully around the bottom half of the biscuit. 'Runners, I reckon. I've always liked runners because you can eat the whole bean.' I ring the Scarlet Emperors in the catalogue.

'Onions?' I ask, looking at a bunch of smooth, papery globes. Dad takes a bite of his biscuit. 'Not worth it. They only cost pence to buy.'

'How about broad beans?' I ask. 'Waste of effort,' says Dad. 'Half your labour goes into growing the pod. You only get a handful of beans at the end of it, then the phone rings while you're cooking 'em and they get burnt to buggery. Bloody washouts if you ask me.'

But I love broad beans and in fact have already planted some Aquadulce, an overwintering variety. When I went to tidy the shed, I saw their first leaves poking up through the soil, a beautiful pistachio green. I look forward to seeing the delicate black and white flowers when they come.

I also admire their growth rate, moderate and steady. They don't alarm with excess leafage like spinach nor turn to marrows overnight like courgettes. Mr MS shares my feeling about rife growth and admits to a mild dread of August because of 'a burgeoning quality' about the plant life. 'Giddying,' he calls it, 'as if something is about to burst.'

But back to the seed catalogue, where I sneak a red ring around the Imperial Longpods and decide that when the time comes, I will enjoy eating them all by myself, slathered in butter and gobbled down in great forkfuls. It is the ugly side of gardening.

Dad and I press on through the catalogue, or rather I suggest options and he vetoes them. Sweet corn, cabbage, peas and beetroot are all summarily dismissed, with relish. He hasn't addressed the envelope to the pendant people nor got up to fetch a stamp. I decide not to remind him. His memory isn't what it is (whose is? – as he might say) so there's every chance that if he puts the still blank white envelope to one side, he'll forget about it altogether.

When I get home, Mr MS is at the stove making himself a bacon, egg and sausage sandwich. I decide to ask him what his favourite vegetable is. Not counting potatoes, I add.

This qualification stymies him for a few minutes.

'Err... peas?' he tries.

'There's no right answer. Just say what you feel.'

Fear enters his eyes. But he rallies. 'All vegetables are different and I like them all for what's individual and special about them.'

'For a man whose top ten films are constantly under revision, that surprises me,' I say.

'Alright,' he says. 'Baked beans.'

I laugh, not at him but because together, the three of us have scored a hat-trick. Be they runners, broadies or tinned haricots, it's clear that we all love beans.

February 2012. Love among the lettuces part III

As you'll no doubt remember, the romance between scarecrow lovers Harry and the Lady of Shallot was blighted by our allotment neighbour who, in the grip of a fantasy about juicy cukes, erected a huge polytunnel between them. We left the Lady bodiless on a shelf in the shed. Nevertheless, as late winter arrives it is yet again very windy and I begin to hope that the polytunnel will flap away, borne on its giant transparent wings. But it doesn't. And then life throws another gigantic spanner in the works.

Harry undergoes gender reassignment.

Now, I am a modern woman. I know that when one falls in love, one falls in love with a person not a gender. And in that sense, nothing has changed. Underneath the tiered skirt and floral jacket that I find Harry wearing one chilly morning at the plot, his face thankfully back in place, he is the same as ever. His soul, or as some might term it his broomstick, hasn't changed. And although the Lady belongs to the century of Alfred Lord Table-Tennyson and probably doesn't share my liberal views, I'm sure she will come round. She will, I hope, stay in love regardless, despite Harry's poor fashion choices. She might even consider a gender change herself and become the Lad of Shallot.

But there's a further problem. Harry has turned into a coke addict. The demure looking headscarf can't hide the straw poking permanently out of his left nostril.

I fumble with the padlock on our shed door, almost forgetting the secret combination. How is the Lady going to take this latest news? When I finally open the door and see her head resting on its shelf, my heart sinks. Losing her body last year was a barrier to romance and no mistake but now her face is a sight too. It's dirty, her hair dishevelled. She has a deranged look. That's probably down to the buzzing: she shared the shed with a wasps' nest last summer and I don't think she has ever recovered. My nerve fails. I can't add to her troubles with this latest news.

135

I need to think. And perhaps I need to think laterally. I stroll around the plot in the way I do at the beginning of any visit, inspecting for progress/damage. When I reach the broad beans, inspiration strikes. I remember something, or rather someone I saw on another plot on the way here. Mr MS is fond of quoting Aristotle's saying, 'one nail knocks out another.' This is particularly true in the area of romance, I decide. I go back into the shed and bundle the Lady's head into a bin-bag. Undignified yes, but sometimes the end justifies the means. I march her quickly to a plot near the entrance gate and pop her head out.

I turn her eyes in the direction of the allotment site's new arrival: Hobby Horse Person. He stands between a compost bin and a water butt, looking handsome in a cerebral kind of way. As we gaze on him, it all makes sense. You and I may see only a head on a pole. But for the Lady, given her current status, I have a hunch that he'll be an inspirational figure, standing as he does for all those who have dispensed with their bodies and its many oppressions for good.

Having feasted our eyes, we walk slowly back to our own plot. When we pass Harry, the Lady doesn't so much as spare him a glance. This is a Good Sign. As I replace her head on its corner shelf next to the Blood, Fish and Bone, her face wears a dreamy look.

At the very least, HHP will have given her the confidence that it's cool to go body free. But she may actually have found a soul mate. As I lock the shed door, I fancy I hear a sigh. But perhaps it is just the wind rustling through the dead leaves.

March 2012. Humanure

In early spring Mr Mandy Sutter, not understanding that I am the designated spiritual member of our household, goes on a meditation retreat.

It is something I've been urging him to do, to combat the stress of his chosen hobby, driving instruction. So I can't explain the strange resentment I feel when he finally goes and breaks all contact with me for ten days, as meditation centres urge you to do, though I have always disobeyed them in this. But Mr MS doesn't even text.

To make matters worse, I find myself unable to meditate while he's away. I obviously need a distraction. And so my thoughts turn quite naturally to the absorbing subject of humanure. It hasn't come completely out of the blue. One chap at our allotments is fascinated by composting. His plot is a-squirm with wormeries and a-pong with buckets of soaking comfrey leaves.

He recently showed me inside his shed, a-ferment with nitrogen fixers and bottles of his own piss that he keeps for experimental amounts of time. It isn't just human piss that interests him. He is keen on dogs' urine too and somehow manages to collect it from passing dogs to put on his compost heap.

One morning it is so sunny and fresh that I manage to persuade Dad to join me at the plot. It is the first time he's been down in ages and he thinks he might paint some preservative on the shed. I am delighted. On the way there we pass compost man, watching his garden shredder cut all his plot waste into tiny pieces so that it composts quicker. I find this encouraging and decide to pop the question.

'Morning,' I say. 'Have you ever thought about a composting toilet? I've been reading up about it online. All you need is a bucket and some sawdust.'

'Hmm.' The man scratches his grizzled chin.

'It's composting with knobs on,' I say.

'I'm sure it is,' he says. 'I'll think about it.'

I suspect he's just being polite.

Dad seems puzzled by our exchange. 'Do you know that fellow?' he asks as we totter on to our own plot.

'Not really,' I say. 'Well, only to talk about bodily excreta to.'

'Huh,' says Dad. I begin to wonder if he might consider setting up a composting toilet in the shed, keen as he is on DIY. He's always been interested in chemicals, which is promising.

'What's your view on it, Dad?' I ask, as I unlock the padlock on the shed, open the door and wind the string around the coat hook.

Dad goes into the shed and extracts an ancient paintbrush and an equally ancient tin of creosote. 'My view on what?'

'You know, setting up a composting toilet in our shed? All we'd need is...'

'A bucket and some sawdust, I heard you.'

He puts the tin down and goes round and round the rusted lid with a screwdriver to prise it off. 'It's the other part of the operation I'm not so keen on.'

'You mean...'

'I mean crapping in a bucket. I don't think we've come to that yet.'

He dips his brush in the tin. I'm pretty sure creosote has been banned for years, but there is no point in telling him this. He'll get angry and use even more of it than he'd planned to, perhaps painting the bench and the tree into the bargain. Also, I'm encouraged by his use of the word 'yet' as regards the composting toilet.

'Ok,' I say. 'Maybe next year then.'

Dad begins daubing the shed. I start weeding a nearby bed but glancing over from time to time I see that although he starts off clumsily, as he works on his painting become more fluid. It's a treat to see him in action again.

As for me, I recognise that it's the old story: I am trying and failing to get males to do something of my choosing, not theirs. I wouldn't mind setting up the actual toilet, but I gather that maintenance is the crucial thing and can make the difference between a toilet's success and failure. And maintenance is the bit I really don't want to do. I must be missing Mr MS.

Luckily, he returns the next day, having left the retreat a day early. He looks radiant: relaxed and ten years younger. I am unsettled by his sudden good looks. 'I've missed you,' I say. 'The upstairs sink got blocked with hair and I couldn't bring myself to fish it out.'

'You look stressed,' he says, 'you need to meditate.'

'How can I, now that you've taken it over?' I cry.

'I think you'll find there are other people in the world who meditate besides me.'

I suppose he's right. And another thing: we do have a small shed in our back yard. Perhaps we could have a composting toilet there. It might be a healing thing. I'll ask Mr MS about the maintenance aspect tomorrow. I'll have to get him off that meditation cushion first, though.

July 2014. Plum crazy

Two years go by and suddenly Dad is 90. 'Well, that crept up on me,' he says. Mr MS buys two gigantic silver skinned helium balloons – a nine and a zero - bringing them home in a black bin bag to stop them floating up into the ozone layer.

'Are you mad?' I ask him. 'Dad will absolutely hate those. He'll think they're hideous and a waste of money.' 'Maybe,' says Mr MS mildly. 'We'll see.'

That afternoon when we go round with cake and card, Dad absolutely loves the balloons and insists on multiple photos with them as the centre piece. He keeps them for weeks, until they are collapsed silver remnants dangling from the ceiling.

A few weeks later still, Mr MS and I move to a new plum tree. The plum tree isn't the main reason for buying the new house, of course. That would be the greenhouse, small and rickety with many cracked and missing panes, but as other gardeners will understand, worth shelling out £300,000 for. There's also a little greengage tree next to the plum which we're told has never borne fruit.

Another reason for moving is the garage. I'm not interested in it from the camper van's point of view but from Dad's: it offers workshop space, something missing from flat life. All his old tools come out of storage and are installed along the top of a lovely old workbench that belonged to the late husband of a kind friend.

Dad gets his own key and is free to come and go as he pleases. And come and go he does. If I see Cheeky Looks parked outside, I bob out to the garage to offer him a cuppa. Engrossed in a project, he is often irritated by the interruption but if I time it right, he sometimes accepts.

As for the tree, it presents us with plum upon plum. In August my kitchen scales register 100lbs worth. Mr MS teeters on a step ladder with a rake and I plum all my new neighbours, even the men who hang around the lockups at the bottom of the lane. Via the fruit, we get to know everyone a little more. One neighbour, who is ten, has been gardening since he was three and has his own greenhouse. We also discover that the people in the other half of our semi don't like plums. What freedoms they must enjoy!

The plums also bring reflection. How salutary it is to receive bounty that one has done nothing to earn! Especially when weeks of back breaking labour at the allotment often produce nothing more than a few handfuls of broad beans and some unimpressive onions.

Being my father's daughter, the thought of waste makes me edgy. So I find myself enslaved to picking, distributing, freezing, jamming and chutneying as well as cake, clafoutis and crumble making. Mr MS no longer listens to sentences that contain the word 'plum' and my trousers grow tight. Dog MS learns to eat windfalls, with colourful results.

As for Dad, he has always loved stewed fruit. Strolling past any autumnal fruit tree that overhangs public land, he never fails to hook the branches down with his walking stick and fill his green nylon shopper with sweet plunder. He's therefore only too happy to receive bags of plums from our tree, throwing them straight into the pan with a kilo of sugar and waving aside my warnings about maggots.

'Maggots won't do you any harm,' he says, or rather shouts, (plum)stone deaf these days and still a hearing aid refusenik. 'After all, what do they eat? Plums, that's what. Maggots are made entirely of plum.'

If I didn't find so many maggots in our plums and if we didn't go round to Dad's house so regularly for tea, I would find this view refreshing. As it is, when the bowl of stewed plums arrives topped by what Dad calls a 'bollio' of vanilla ice cream, I can't help examining it for the grey crescent shaped creatures that, once cooked, look so much like toenail clippings. Boiled alive, imagine it! As so often at Dad's, I resort to a surreptitious approach, enjoying my bollio but transferring purple spoonfuls into Mr MS's bowl when Dad isn't looking. 'Steady on!' hisses Mr MS. But he is nothing if not tactful and, as calculated, stops short of exposing my misdeed.

But back to gardening. French gardener, botanist and writer Gilles Clement, known for his design of public parks, wrote, 'All management generates an abandoned area.' Wise words that make me wonder what area of my life is now abandoned because of obsessive plum management. If I let the fruit rot on the tree, would there be benefits in other areas? And would those areas be more or less valid? I used to throw my hands up in horror at a local Bramley tree, gravid with apples that the owners never picked. I wonder now if they had other areas of life they weren't prepared to abandon in service of stewed fruit. Perhaps they were more spiritually evolved than I, though that is hard to imagine. I resolve to ask Mr MS about this. If you've ever wondered what goes on behind closed doors at our house it is discussions like this, accompanied by a nice cup of tea and a plum flapjack.

Before I have to face up to a full examination of my life's priorities, however, the plums begin to slow down. Ah, I can delay the moment of truth until next year! Or can I? Unfortunately, the greengage tree is fruiting for the first time this year, and that fruit is starting to ripen.

THE PLUMS IN THE HALLWAY...

Part 3 – The Last Years

July 2016. Projects

Two years pass. Fish and chips nights carry on, as do regular coffees and visits to the plot, sometimes with Dad, sometimes without. Mr MS remains the only one of us who can visit the allotment for pleasure and not with a task in mind. He achieves this by keeping himself in a state of ignorance and therefore bliss about what needs doing. He will do as he is told, but over the past years has resisted absorbing information permanently. It is like dealing with a goldfish. Even Dog MS takes more responsibility, making sure always to guard the back fence and bark at the wheelbarrow.

In 2016, I am in the running for a literary award. When I make the long list, Dad is beside himself. He spends a frustrating hour with the photocopier in the local library, trying to copy newspaper mentions to send to family friends and relatives. When I'm shortlisted, he decides to invest in a colour printer. He spends hours fiddling about with different sorts of paper and every time I go for coffee he has new versions of the coverage. 'What do you think about THIS one?' he urges. 'The colours are a bit muted on your picture but the wording is easier to read.'

When I am named the winner at the ceremony, as soon as I decently can I dash outside to ring him. He is ecstatic. 'You WON!' he keeps saying. 'You actually WON.' An email, in capital letters, goes straight out to family friends and relatives. 'SHE WON!!'

I am delighted to win the award, of course. But I am also delighted by Dad's delight. When, a month later, he suffers a DVT and develops a leg ulcer and cellulitis (to do, we gather, with poor circulation and his elderly heart) I am glad we had such an exultant summer.

Walking becomes even more difficult for him than before, especially on uneven ground. His leg falls to the care of the District Nurses, who visit him regularly to bandage it. I buy him a Rollator, which in theory he could pop into the boot of Cheeky Looks (yes, at 93 he is still driving) and take to the allotment gates, as he hasn't visited the plot in ages. He gives it a brief try but pronounces it 'too fast. 'Did you use the brakes?' I ask. 'I didn't realise it had brakes,' he says. I perk up, thinking this new intel will encourage him to try afresh. But somehow The Rollator's moment never comes again.

He also refuses to use a stick. With his disabled parking badge, he can park next to the trolleys at Tesco's and from there hang on to one all the way round the store.

Unlike the Rollator, I note, trolleys have no brakes, but this doesn't seem to worry him. Sometimes he whizzes around in their motorized shopper. In his flat, he works his way around by steadying himself on occasional tables.

One morning, finding the Rollator dumped near his wheelie bin, I realise it was a mistake to interfere. That's primarily because, while Dad's loss of mobility gets him down, it has also become his new project. He's happy to leave my projects, like writing, up to me. By the same token, he's not keen on me sticking my oar into his. He prefers to steer by his own lights. I will do well to remember it.

October 2016. Morrisongate

Later in the year, something happens that casts doubt on Dad's driving. I accept a lift from him to a town about ten miles away, which has a Sainsbury's. He says their navel oranges are thinner skinned and juicier than Tesco's and they also have Orange Club biscuits on offer for £1. It being the right time of year for buying bulbs and overwintering onion sets, I am happy to go along. I might even buy something for tea. I think it will be nice to drive with Dad for the first time in years. But I've got another think coming.

For starters, Dad drives with his seat unnervingly far forward so that his chest almost touches the steering wheel. This cuts down his side vision. And even his forward vision is questionable – he peers through the windscreen as if through torrential rain. He is also given to unpredictable and as far as I can see unnecessary braking. I bite my tongue, quite literally. By the time we arrive at Sainsbury's my mouth is full of blood. Feeling queasy, I rush to the ladies. When I come out, my tongue tender and lumpy, I can see Dad, unmistakeable with his red face, tweed cap and anorak, having a ding dong with a shop assistant at the store entrance. His legendary 'up and downers' are becoming more common.

In a sort of panic, I duck back into the ladies to wash my hands again, soaping right up to the wrists. I dry my hands elaborately on dozens of paper towels, then anoint my lips several times with lip salve. By the time I emerge there's thankfully no sign of Dad.

Forgetting whatever it was I wanted to buy I sit behind the checkouts and wait for him. When he appears ten minutes later, I wave but he doesn't see me. As he checks his few items through the till a lump comes to my throat. He looks every bit as frail and bent and shuffly as one might expect. But more poignantly he seems locked inside an inner world that doesn't look much fun. I wonder if this trip is proving too much for him. I feel guilty and resolve to be extra helpful for the rest of the day.

My resolve crumbles almost immediately, not during our uneventful walk back to the car, but during what comes after it. Dad, not mentioning his argument in Sainsbury's, announces that he'd like to fill up Cheeky Looks at Morrison's garage. He has checked out the prices and their petrol is the cheapest for twenty miles around.

'Good idea,' I say, bracing myself for another stint of terrifying passengerhood.

We manage the short drive to the garage without incident and pull up at a front pump. 'I'll do this, Dad,' I say, jumping out of the car before he has a chance to object. I fill Cheeky up and go into the shop to pay. When I come back, the woman at the pump behind us is finishing up and crossing the forecourt to the shop.

We agreed beforehand on a visit to a cafe I know and like. But now he pulls a face at the idea. 'I think we'll just go home love, shall we? We can have a cuppa there. And a nice chocolate biscuit. And it'll be free.'

I'm surprised at how morose I suddenly feel at being denied my cappuccino. I'm not sure whether it's Dad's increasing frailty talking, or his lifelong habit of getting his own way. Either way there's only one possible course of action. 'Whatever you like,' I say, letting the comforting thought of a coffee plus crisp mini butter shortbread float away.

He nods, switches on the ignition and puts Cheeky into gear. But instead of going forwards, we kangaroo violently back. There is one hell of a bang and we stall. I realise we've hit the car behind.

Waiting for people to stream across the forecourt shouting, especially the woman whose car it is, I turn to Dad. 'Dad! I think you've...' But he is starting the car again and putting it in gear. 'Stop!' I say. 'You hit that car.'

He pulls away from the petrol pump with a loud squeal of tyres. 'Dad! Didn't you feel it?' I say. 'We can't just...'

But it's too late. We're already turning back onto the main road, causing a car to brake suddenly to avoid us. I glance back at the garage. The woman is out from the shop now, approaching her car. Dad is locked again into his grim world. And in a re-enactment of the Sainsbury's scene, while we speed past the garage I find myself trying to escape, sliding down in my seat and hunching my shoulders as if it really was possible to make myself invisible.

October 2017. Rustic woodwork

Another year passes. How they fly! Dad limps on but begins to drive less. I am heartily relieved and also glad that he doesn't dwell on the loss, preferring to imagine that he's going to get back behind the wheel when his leg gets better.

We are all getting on a bit. Mr MS and I seem to be talking more about ageing, in ourselves ('I can't carry more than three things out to the car without dropping one of them!' he reveals one day) but even more in Dad, now 94 and Dog MS, now 10.

Likewise, the cheap bench that Mr MS assembled once upon a time and Dad mended has now put in a lot of outdoor years and is looking ropey. Rather than make another uninspiring purchase at B&Q, I decide I'd like to make a new bench myself. Making furniture is in my blood of course. Dad and his Dad before him made all the tables, chairs and monstrous sideboards in their respective homes. I mean, how hard can it be? I find a beginner's woodwork course running locally in November and December.

On the first day I'm alarmed to see that the other participants are all male and at least thirty years younger than me. Some have care workers with them. And from the way the organizer talks to me in a loud, slow voice, she obviously thinks I have learning difficulties. I should have smelt a rat when the application form asked me if the course would help me cope better with daily life. But writers are compelled to craft careful replies to all questionnaires. So I described in detail (with examples) how gardening and other practical hobbies helped me deal with stress. There was supposed to be a waiting list for the course but I was offered a place immediately.

I survive the first day despite discovering a sobering fact: when people treat you as though you have learning difficulties, you start having learning difficulties. I commit a ridiculous number of what the French term 'betises.' The drill wobbles in my grasp and screws go in aslant. I gouge ugly chunks out of my 'project' with the chisel. I try to use the plane upside down and wonder why no wood shavings come out.

Lovely Tom, roofer turned tutor, corrects me gently. He is a gifted, patient teacher with a sense of humour and a knack of being there just before someone lops their fingers off with the circular saw or gets dragged across the workshop floor by the belt sander. I catch myself hoping he sees me as 'normal', whatever that means.

But in the end the question of who has 'issues' and who hasn't is irrelevant. All the group are better at woodwork than me. And they are all fatherly despite their youth. They steady planks while I saw wonkily and hold my project while I try to hammer nails in straight. One even tries to give me the bedside cabinet he has spent five weeks making. Tom gently discourages him. My bench turns out well (it is only a basic one) and I have time to make an allotment gate out of old pallet wood. Back at home the weekend after the course finishes, I even knock up some cross supports for the raspberry canes I planted last year and install them. They make the plot look like a site of religious pilgrimage. We cut some chicken wire away between two of Dad's uprights and Mr MS helps me hang the new gate in the gap. Then I paint it in yellow preservative and screw a brass number 2 into the top. We have a gate at last, and it looks fantastic. I feel mightily chuffed to have made some of our allotment accoutrements with my own hand and I photograph everything, with plenty of close ups, to show Dad the following morning.

Once the coffee has come in safely to land on the coffee table, he scrolls through the shots on my phone. 'This gate,' he says, jabbing his finger on the screen in a way that makes the picture zoom in, zoom out then disappear. I extract the phone from his grip and reinstate the picture.

'Yes?' I say, readying myself for a compliment. But he is scowling. 'You've used far too many screws. Have you got money to burn?' I am taken aback. 'Well... no. But the screws were the only cost. The wood came from an old pallet and cost nothing.'

He isn't mollified. 'So why spend everything you've saved on screws? Especially when nails would have done the job just as well.' 'They only cost a few quid,' I say. 'Yes, but it's the principle of the thing,' he says.

153

What about the principle of your daughter wanting to follow in your footsteps, I almost say. Now his approval is being withheld, I realise that I've been hoping to impress him.

'I could have done that,' he mutters, and switches the BBC news channel on, something to which he seems increasingly addicted.

All through the loud drumbeats and portentously spoken headlines, my cheeks burn with injustice and disappointment. It strikes me that Dad is viewing my woodworking efforts as an attempt to usurp his role, and a poor attempt at that. I wonder too if he feels I've defied him by installing a gate.

There is nothing to do but drink my coffee. For a change I actually eat my Jacob's Club Orange biscuit instead of pretending to. I'm in luck: it's only slightly stale. As the news rumbles heavily on, doing its best to bludgeon us into despair, I can even see that Dad is right about one thing. My attitude is not that of a master craftswoman. My slogan is 'that'll do.' I'm happy if people can sit on my rustic bench without getting a splinter up their backsides.

By the time news gives way to weather, I have also realised that although this is a lowly goal, it's enough for me. If my gate falls apart in a year, I will make another one. In fact, I will enjoy making another one. I may decide to do it slightly differently, though there's no way I'm going to use nails instead of screws.

Dad always makes enough coffee for me to have a second cup, even though he only ever drinks one himself. I get up to fetch the cafetiere. He sits on, riveted to the screen.

I enjoy a calming potter in his kitchen, free of the grim force field in the next room. Then I take a few deep breaths and go back to my chair to face whatever comes next. On the way I pass the sideboard that Dad made himself. On it, he keeps nine little blocks of different woods, planed and polished to show the grain. He often stands, as best he can at 93, and turns them over in his hands. And smiles.

I think I am beginning to understand why.

January 2018. Hot beds

The joy of allotment-related learning has inspired me. As soon as the dust settles on the woodwork course, I enrol on another local offering taking place at the end of January: The Ancient Art of the Hot Bed. We've had the allotment for seven years now, and I could use a refreshment to my way of doing things.

We have got Christmas out of the way. On the day, always difficult for Dad, he talked at some length about how much he loathes January and February. Perhaps many elderly people feel this way, but his words only made me realise how much I look forward to these cold but bracing months all through the darkling days of November and December. And the thought of the hotbed course makes me look forward to them even more.

To clarify, these are not the kind of hotbeds you read about in the Daily Mail. They are the sort that people have been constructing since the year 200 BC in pursuit of the gardeners' Holy Grail: the extension of the growing season. With a hotbed, you can start growing vegetables as soon as there is a decent amount of daylight around. In other words, in January and February instead of the more standard April and May.

The day – a perishing one – finally arrives. The course is run by Jack First, the UK's foremost hotbed expert, who lives – amazingly – in a town ten miles from ours. At his extensive allotments, under his instruction, eight of us, swaddled up in coats, gloves, scarves and hats, make a hotbed. We take a big slatted compost bin and stuff it with fresh manure. Jack says that when we come to make our own hotbeds, we can use anything organic that's already part rotted. I mentally earmark some ancient cotton underpants I saw drying in Dad's bathroom and some disreputable jeans that belong to Mr MS. We put a cold frame on top and fill it with compost. Then we plant seeds.

These seeds apparently will go off like billy-o, turbo charged with the steady warmth from the decomposing pants, etc. In winter, slugs and snails are still a-slumber in the soil, so the produce – lettuce in February, spinach in

March, carrots in April – won't be attacked by pests and will come out glossy and hyper real, like in a TV gardening programme. And by the following winter the whole contents of the hotbed will have turned to compost, ready to be used as the growing medium in next year's hotbed.

It is a thing of beauty. Jack leads us through a series of polytunnels, which he has effectively turned into hotbed houses. Frost abounds outside but inside it is so warm that we all take off our woolly hats and gloves. We drink our coffee and witness tomato and lettuce seedlings coming through. You can almost see them growing. I am completely sold on the idea, and buy Jack's book.

The only difficulty will be procuring sufficient quantities of manure, heavy stuff to lug around. I realise I will need to start grooming Mr Mandy Sutter (who has shown prowess in the manure department once before) immediately.

'We could go to the allotment tomorrow,' I say as I walk through the front door. 'How nice that would be, to get out into the fresh air after being cooped up in the house all winter.'

He looks up from the joyless philosophy tome he forced me to buy him for Christmas. 'Cooped up is good,' he says. 'Fresh air is overrated.'

'Is that what Schopenhauer says?' I ask. Then I deliver the killer blow. 'I think we've still got some plums in the freezer. I could make that lovely plum, hazelnut and chocolate cake. We could have it with our flask.'

His expression changes. 'Oh well, if you put it like that...' he says.

The following morning, once he is wellied-up, it is child's play to lever him into the camper van. Inside, he smells a rat. 'What are those carrier bags for? And that spade?'

'It's good to be prepared,' I say. That's surely the kind of statement Schopenhauer makes, or would do if he had any sense.

'Prepared for what?' asks Mr MS.

I let the question hang: the doors are locked and we are already caning it down the A65 towards the local stables.

At the stables, we stare at sky high piles, some steaming, some glittering with frost.

'What the...?' says Mr MS.

I talk of the steaming pile he'll see in April, of new potatoes slathered in butter. I say that although Dad's status as a grower is diminishing, his status as an eater remains strong and he'll love the runner beans that will climb down the sides of the bed after the early crops finish.

Mr MS looks at me. Manipulation, shaming and emotional blackmail are my middle name, he knows. But it's his kindness that makes him go along with me. He picks up a carrier bag. I hand him a spade.

'Get shovelling that shit,' I murmur. He laughs. He loves it when I talk dirty.

February 2018. A friend in swede

Late winter is here. The hotbed is set up, and I'm excited to see radish seedlings already coming up in it, just as Jack said they would. On the rest of the plot, the winter crops planted last year are still going. We have perennial kale, which produces nearly all year round (a blessing of course, but as noted elsewhere, it's amazing how familiarity breeds contempt) and also swedes, which I've grown for the first time this winter and which are doing a bit too well for my liking.

The difficulty is getting anyone to eat either of these noble and health-giving vegetables. This problem has got worse as the years have gone by, the novelty of home-grown veg having now worn off completely. Everyone has retreated back into their comfort zone. When it's Mr MS's turn to cook, he goes to Tesco's for his veg, just as he used to in pre-allotment days. I find a shrink-wrapped head of broccoli on the kitchen counter, alongside an extortionately priced four pack of baking potatoes.

'Why buy broccoli when there's all that kale to eat?' I want to know when he comes back in. 'And we've still got potatoes left in the garage. Plus there's all that swede. We need to start making inroads on it soon!' My frustration, naturally, is sharpened by fierce envy. If only I could go to Tesco's to buy broccoli! And Mr MS, having hoped for some brownie points for making the tea, looks dismayed. He shuffles the innocent potatoes into the fridge.

'The ones in the garage take too long to peel,' he says. 'They're small and most of them are full of worms. And where's all this kale and swede you keep talking about?'

'Where do you think they are? At the allotment!'

'You mean, I'd have to go down there and get them?' His face is a picture. It's no good blaming the chill weather: he was the same in summer. Later that afternoon when I come back with a gigantic swede, he's still not convinced. 'But it's all covered in muck!' he exclaims. Then he says he's forgotten how to make swede mash, even though I've told him countless times.

Dad is no better. When I lifted my admittedly poor rainbow carrots last autumn, he stared at their purple, white and yellow hues and said, 'Don't expect me to eat those. I like my carrots orange.'

And he has never eaten a single root veg from the plot apart from potatoes. 'Isn't that the stuff they feed cattle?' he asks when I try to slip him a swede. 'Anyway I'm on salads at the moment.' A likely story. Who but a raw food zealot would be eating salads in February? I leave it a week then present him with another one, so much smaller that it is almost cute. He eyes the knobbly form. 'The thing is, love,' he says, 'I've adopted a new regime. I breakfast like a king, lunch like a lord and dine like a pauper. Swede doesn't really fit in.' A cry escapes me. Such is my despair that for once I'm letting my real feelings show. He relents. 'Alright, I'll give it a go. I suppose I could try a stew tomorrow.'

Over the next week I make polite enquiries every time I ring, but Dad refuses to be drawn on the subject of either the stew or the swede. 'It's in the fridge,' is all he will say. 'I chip bits off it now and then.' This approach may have its merits but it won't make much impact on the twenty fat swedes lolling around down at the plot.

Needless to say, both Dad and Mr MS enjoy swede and even kale when it has been picked, cleaned, chopped and incorporated into a delicious casserole by someone else, especially if gravy and dumplings are involved. Or cream. Which isn't my dream of allotmenteering. Not only do I have to grow the bloody vegetables, I have to cook them too. Hoping for romance, I once asked Mr MS what he liked best about me. 'Your stews,' he said. Another dream shattered.

Thank goodness for Dog MS, a quick learner when it comes to food. When offered grapes on a stalk, she quickly learnt how to pull them off one by one, rather gently, with her teeth. Later she discovered how to mount the settee and take the whole bunch out of the fruit bowl, but that's another story. With blackberries she watched me pick them a few times then was out in the garden picking them herself.

I take her down to the plot, secure in the knowledge that vegetables don't have to be cooked for her to enjoy them. They don't have to be cleaned. They don't even have to be dug up. She plonks herself down in the middle of my root veg bed, digs up a swede and wedges it between her front paws. Then she begins grating it with her fore-teeth. The sound strikes me as charming. Interesting to reflect that if Dad or Mr MS were reproducing it at the dinner table I would find it infuriating.

Happily, dogs' teeth aren't designed for swede and this relaxing sound makes for a companionable hour together. What a delight! And I can't help feeling proud. One always hopes that one's child substitute will inherit one's own values.

March 2018. Infamy, infamy

Now that the daffs are coming out – a joyous sight – Dad keeps going off into a chorus of Odgen Nash. 'Spring is sprung/the grass is riz/I wonder where the boidies is?' Any mention of the Arab Spring triggers the same response.

He is an enthusiastic custodian of old sayings and catchphrases, inserting them into conversation with relish no matter how irrelevant. 'Shurely shome mishtake,' he says, rerunning the old Private Eye joke every time the TV subtitles slip up.

At the word 'infamous' he channels Kenneth Williams in Carry on Cleo. 'Infamy, infamy, they've all got it infamy.' And if anyone mentions youth he always says, in a cod New York accent, 'at my age, everyone's young.' Then he laughs his head off as though it's the first time anyone's ever heard it.

This isn't an age thing. As long ago as his forties, he repeated the same jokes over and over. When we lived in Kent and I was seven, he used to walk me to the school bus stop every morning. Our route lay along a busy road and the pavement was narrow. He would keep me on the inside, one hand holding tight to his, the other clutching the 2p bus fare. 'This is a very dangerous pavement,' he would say, 'a very, very dangerous pavement.' He would say it again, then after a short pause, again. The incessant repetition was meant to be funny; was funny, though even at seven, I remember a dutiful feeling accompanying my laughter. Perhaps even then I longed for a more meaningful connection with my Dad.

Mr Mandy Sutter, on the other hand, has no problem with Dad's repetitions. For one thing, he is more generous spirited than I am and for another he has only known Dad for 20 years rather than 60. He laughs like a drain and says afterwards that it is great to see Dad enjoying himself.

It's true that we need to make the most of Dad's good moods: he is having a lot of bad ones. Declining health is multiplying his bugbears. He particularly hates having to stay in for the District Nurses, who come three times a week and are never able to give an exact time. He finds some of the nurses tolerable but there are two he can't stand and he insults them to their face, calling one 'a mountain of flesh' and informing the other that she has 'great big thumbs' which she digs into his leg on purpose while bandaging it. He gets her so flustered that one day she trips over and steps right onto his bad foot. He tells her never to darken his (expletive deleted) door again, an expression coined by Benjamin Franklin in 1729. Dog MS has a little crocodile sticker on her file at the vet's and I suspect that the District Nurses' folder will now bear something similar.

So I am beginning to come round to Mr MS's way of thinking: if Dad's in a good enough mood to crack a terrible joke, I should be grateful.

But then, Mr MS would think that way, since he has a fat portfolio of stock phrases himself. One of his chief jokes is answering 'yes please' to a question that merely requires a 'yes' such as 'are you going into Leeds tomorrow?' Of questions that require a 'no' he often says, 'no, no, no, no, no.'

Over the years I have put in some serious graft in the smiling and laughing department, just as I did and still do with Dad. It has often been through gritted teeth as I witness the failure of yet another of my earnest attempts to communicate. Of course, when one's nearest and dearest gives joke answers something IS being communicated, but let's not dwell on that.

It isn't just a gender issue. Mum too was sidetracked by questions of language, though it took a different turn with her. As a heartbroken teenager I'd be confiding in her about a relationship breakup and she'd say 'don't use words like 'dumped' dear! Where do you pick up these vulgar Americanisms?'

I have to say that I'm not entirely innocent myself. Whenever a pig gets referred to or when I see one in real life, I have to squeal 'Piggyyyy!' at high volume. When the three pigs appeared at our allotments a few years ago, this became quite debilitating and even the uber-tolerant Mr MS counselled me to rein it in.

And like Mum I too often long to correct people's speech. The other day a friend said 'summink' instead of 'something'. The effort of trying not to correct her 'brought me out in a muck sweat' (as Dad would say) and I totally lost the thread of the conversation. I'm sure she was telling me summink important. And then she asked me a question. 'Are you going to Leeds tomorrow?' 'Yes please,' I replied.

Early April 2018. The leg

Mid spring arrives and Dad's leg becomes too infected for the District Nurses' liking. They call the doctor, who is young and female and arrives wearing a summery dress and cardigan. She examines the leg while Dad sits in his arm chair. I can see him battling between old school courtesy and equally old school suspicion at her youth, gender and lovely yellow flowery frock.

When she marks his leg with a black miracle marker and takes a photo of it, suspicion triumphs and he explodes. 'Is this a joke?'

'No,' she says mildly, 'just a simple way to track the spread of your infection.'

'You know nothing!' he bellows. 'How can you? You're just a school kid!'

I freeze, but the doctor doesn't flinch, just very gently re-bandages his leg.

'I'm so, so sorry,' I say in Dad's hallway. 'He gets very worked up. He feels powerless, I think.'

'Totally understandable,' she says. 'And how about you?' She touches my upper arm. 'Are you coping okay?'

I jump back as if stung. Is she trying to get me onto anti-depressants? 'I'm fine,' I say, far more curtly than I mean to. As I show her out, I thank her excessively to make up for it. She must think we're a right pair. When I return to the sitting room, Dad's face is a mask of anguish. 'I expect I'll lose the leg. They'll have to amputate.'

'Oh, Dad,' I say, squeezing his arm. 'Have you been looking things up on the Internet again? I doubt it'll come to that.'

I go to make a cup of tea and give him time to calm down. And calm down he does. 'Don't worry about me,' he says gamely, as I come back in with the tea. 'My other leg is perfectly good. I'm sure I can learn to can manage with just the one.'

When the doctor visits again a few days later the redness has travelled a good inch above the black line. 'You could do with some intravenous antibiotics, Ted,' she says. 'How would you feel about being admitted to hospital? I can arrange an ambulance for this afternoon. We need to get on top of this infection.'

'Ted?' he says, 'Ted? I'll thank you to call me by my full name.'

It is a worrying development. But my first and extremely trivial thought is that I'd better take back the early pickings of allotment lettuce that I've put in Dad's fridge and we'll have it for tea tonight, perhaps with a nice quiche. My second thought is that I have a work commitment this afternoon which involves filming. It isn't something I can miss. I dither then ring Mr MS, who is luckily free this afternoon and says he will sit with Dad until the ambulance arrives.

Dad is disgusted by this plan. 'Filming? How can you go off to be FILMED at a time like this?'

I feel awful. 'Look Dad, the doctor thinks it's only a routine visit. And I'll be back in three hours. I'll come straight to the hospital.'

'I'll probably be dead by then,' he says. I stare at him then go out into the hall to ring Mr MS again, who can always be relied upon to pour oil on the troubled waters of our family dynamics. 'He's just upset,' he says. 'He'll be perfectly alright. I'll come up now and have a word with him.' Mr MS is an absolute brick. We change shifts and I say I'll ring him every half hour for updates.

In the event, the ambulance takes three hours to arrive. Filming done and dusted, I arrive at the hospital before either of them. I ring Mr MS from hospital reception. He has packed Dad's overnight bag and found some news coverage of a recent earthquake on Sky, which has calmed Dad down immensely. 'He's much more resigned now,' says Mr MS. 'He's even saying he supposes things like this are only to be expected when you're 93 and three quarters.'

The tears that have been waiting in the background all day spring to my eyes and I have to visit the Ladies for a few muted sobs and a nose blow. Then I dry my eyes and go to get a cup of tea before the cafe closes.

Late April 2018. Sir Dad

Dad is kept in hospital for three weeks, until the end of the month. Turns out it's harder to get out than it was to get in. They move him from ward to ward and finally to a rehab unit where he is encouraged to walk as much as possible and, in a dummy kitchen, assessed by an OT on his ability to make a cup of tea. 'What a joke,' he says. 'I've been making cups of tea since before she was born.'

He is shepherded daily into a day room to participate in armchair aerobics. 'Waving your arms about?' he queries. 'What good does that do anyone?'

We visit him every day, of course. Approaching his bed bay, you often hear him before you see him. 'What the bloody hell do you think you're doing?' is his battle cry. The blue curtains around his bed tremble. When the curtains are open and he can see the other patients in the bed bay, he tends to voice loud opinions about them. 'That poor bugger over there has had his leg amputated. He'll be lucky if he lasts the night.'

'The NHS is fucking useless!' he shouts at a nurse when his painkillers are late arriving. His language is getting worse. 'I can't disagree with that,' she says.

In his diary he's compiling a list of names, under the heading 'Incompetent Staff – Complaint.' Mr MS and I, sensitive types, are mortified and apologetic. We imagine he's a nightmare patient.

So it's a surprise to arrive on another visit to find a young healthcare assistant clasping Dad's hand in hers and telling him she loves him. 'You remind me of my grandfather back in Hungary,' she says. 'He too has a problem in the leg.'

The feeling seems to be mutual. 'My friend,' Dad tells her, his eyes brimming. 'My only ally in this terrible place!'

Dad has also clicked with a young male healthcare assistant who is interested in astronomy and has been to NASA. Dad asks us to bring in the old Carl Sagan book *Cosmos* that he's had for decades. He presents it to the lad, who is very touched. When we bump into him in the corridor later, he says of Dad, 'some patients you know you'll never forget.'

This puts me in mind of something one of the District Nurses told me last month. 'To be honest, we prefer a character. Your Dad tells it like it is. Can't be doing with them as just sits there and won't say boo to a goose.'

This isn't the only encouraging news. Towards the end of Dad's stay, following an impressive performance on the Zimmer fame, he gets christened Speedy Ted. Someone makes him a special cardboard sign and attaches it to his frame. The rehab unit allows us to visit with fish and chips, and to bring Dog MS in up the fire escape for a pat and a saucer of milky tea. I bring in crumble made with allotment rhubarb and it's almost like Sunday night at ours, except that our session in front of the TV is replaced by wheeling Dad up and down eerie corridors then taking him for a coffee at the in-house Costa. He likes the thin wooden stirrers. He breaks them in half to make them sharp then hoards them in his bedside cabinet to use as tooth picks.

Nevertheless, he is desperate to get back home. Before he can be discharged though, he has one more hoop to jump through: a mental health

169

assessment. After it has been done, a young man rings me. 'Ted is mentally very sharp,' he says. 'We chatted about his daily three-mile walks and his digging down at his allotment.'

I am taken aback. 'Three miles? Maybe that was true five years ago, but...'

'And he's keen to get back behind the wheel. He told me how much he enjoys popping to his workshop in your garage to make his furniture.'

'The workshop? Right. Though again, he...' 'Ted has a remarkable life for someone who's nearly 94.'

'Indeed he does,' I say, with as much irony as I can inject into three words. I don't know whether Dad is misremembering his capabilities or lying on purpose. Either way, he is discharged the next day, complete with a huge white paper bag full of medication. Once we're in the car, I check to make sure it's all present and correct. It wouldn't be the first time he has been given the wrong tablets. But everything is in order. Then I notice the label on the outside of the bag. It says Sir Ted.

In the coming days and weeks, the appellation Sir will also appear on medication dispensed by the local pharmacy and in the District Nurses' notes. I'm not clear as to when exactly his knighthood was conferred, but I must say it doesn't seem out of place.

Early May 2018. Of leeks and potatoes

Once Dad is home and back in the care of the District Nurses, I start thinking about the allotment again. It is sunny most days and the plot is a lovely airy place to be after spending hours in stifling hospital bed bays trying not breathe in. I try to recruit Dad for a visit, but he says, 'that place is the least of my worries.'

I start going there at 6.30am to brew up my morning 'boil' and to water. One tap serves many plots and it's in high demand from 7.00am onwards. It is wonderful being there early in the season and early in the morning, a double whammy if ever there was one. All the crops on the plot look dew-fresh and neat. The broad beans' shy black and white flowers offer a delicate scent and the potato tops look perfect, like crinkled dark green paper. Later on in the season there will be rust and blight, but let's not get real just yet.

I feel useful too, something I don't feel trying to help Dad. Potatoes need plenty of water and I can give it to them. I can thereby fulfil my duty to safeguard the Desperate Dan-style piles of mash that Mr MS so enjoys making and eating.

But there's one crop that my watering fails to save.

For several springs now, I have sown leek seeds in trays. They germinate well but even when left for weeks never reach the 'pencil-thick' status that Monty Don recommends. They get to 'spaghetti-thick' and stay there. Harvesting them (sometimes up to a year later) they are still hardly bigger than spring onions. I have kept trying though because both Dad and Mr MS enjoy a nice leek and I enjoy slicing them up – so much more convenient, shape wise, than onions.

In March and April this year I went the extra mile, applying wood ash, saved from our winter fireplace, to their roots and humming *Cwm Rhondda* to them.

171

Unfortunately, even after all this in early May we get a few very hot days and the leeks bolt. Their soft, pale green layers, so delicious when fried with bacon, are pushed outwards and finally replaced by a hard white central stalk. I pick a few to see if there is anything to be salvaged, but the pickings are slim indeed. I'm so disappointed that I can't bring myself to talk to the leeks for a week, let alone sing to them. I just pretend they aren't there and start talking to the potato plants instead.

But while my back is turned, a miracle happens. They all shoot up to 5' high and produce seed heads shaped like minarets. So spectacular a sight they make, like a blue-green Istanbul, that I waste hours of watering time sitting on my bench gazing. I find excuses to pass among them and allow their heavy smooth heads to knock lazily against my back and shoulders.

Another allotmenteer tells me that left to their own devices, they will naturalise. Leeklets will spring up around their bases and seed from their flower heads will fall and germinate in situ. Now I'm sure all gardeners would love a green crop that looks after itself the way, say, rhubarb does, producing lovely food while we stand by barely lifting a finger. But I can't see it actually happening. I pretend to believe it though, partly because you should never say never and partly because it gives me an excuse not to deal with the leek bed now.

Of course, there's another crop that excels at naturalisation: every year, alongside yielding a few pounds of decent sized tubers, potato plants always produce a few that are too small to detect with the naked eye. At harvest time, they slip through the tines of the garden fork back into the soil and live to sprout again.

In spring and early summer, making an effort to rotate your crops, you plant out delicate beetroot and lettuce seedlings in your erstwhile potato bed. But over the coming weeks, the rufty tufty dark green rosettes break through again and again, shouldering aside the lettuce and beet, until you give up pulling them out and settle for yet another potato bed. This, of course, is their master plan.

©JANIS GOODMAN 2021

The 'volunteers' (as they are apparently known) are sprouting like crazy in the compost heap this year, too. One early morning before the kettle boils, I decide to dig a few up to see where they've come from. I discover that they are sprouting not from last year's rejected spuds as I imagined, but from a host of potato peelings Mr MS brought down here after preparing one of his huge pans of mash. I had no idea potatoes were so enterprising. I'm impressed, I admit.

Mid-May 2018. Purple pills

When Dad said the allotment was the least of his worries, he was right. Later in the month, he's pulled in to hospital again, then again in early June. By the autumn he will have notched up six hospitalizations of varying lengths as medics battle to get 'on top of the leg.'

But back to his third (evening) admission, when a rather striking consultant, with long grey hair and a goatee beard, visits his bed. He is wearing a bright embroidered waistcoat and a red bow tie. I wonder if he has been summoned from a posh dinner. He examines Dad and announces, 'I see before me a fit 94-year-old man.' He waves his arms around. 'A small problem with the leg, yes. Unsurprising, as it has been kept bandaged.'

'Is this a dagger I see before me?' he goes on. Well, not really, but he projects his next words with force, as though wanting to make sure they reach even the cheapskates sitting up in the Gods. 'What this leg needs is AIR. And the regular application of good old-fashioned iodine.'

The two ward nurses behind him exchange glances. 'Where the fuck are we going to get iodine?' they're probably thinking. I'm dismayed on a different count. 'But the District Nurses have been bandaging his leg for months,' I say.

'Then those nurses don't know what they're doing,' he pronounces, and swans off to get ready for his next performance.

One of the nurses lets out an exasperated huff. 'He shouldn't have said that about the DNs, he really shouldn't. And you can't expose an open wound to air. It's just dangerous.'

But us civvies have been charmed by the extravagantly waist-coated raconteur. His advice represents a change. As Dad says later, 'it isn't as if the bandaging is working, is it?' And when he's visited the next morning by a bespectacled, balding and far less handsome consultant, who throws his hands up in horror at the idea of exposing an already infected leg to hospital germs,

174

none of us are impressed. I consult Doctor Internet about wound exposure protocol and, imagining that we are now well informed, make an appointment to explain ours and Dad's concerns.

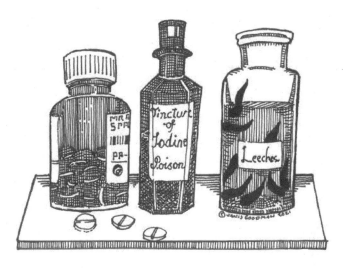

However much of a flipping nuisance the ward staff find us, they are very professional and considered and the appointment goes well. In the coming months bandaging will win hands down, by the sheer token that it's the protocol the District Nurses follow and they're the ones Dad sees most, but for now it's agreed to go back to the advice of the first consultant and expose the leg for a week, bathing it not with iodine but with the more readily available potassium permanganate, or 'pot per.'

We are all pleased. The days go on and the leg begins to show an improvement. But the potassium permanganate comes in tablets which are dissolved in warm water and towards the end of the week, Dad somehow gets hold of some of these highly toxic items and tries to swallow them. Luckily they taste bitter and he spits them out.

He then threatens to sue the hospital. I am called and asked to pick him up immediately. I cancel my day. 'They tried to poison me!' he shouts as soon as I enter the bed bay.

When I ask what actually happened, I am taken into the sister's office and fobbed off with a practised air. I read between the lines. A nurse was called away while doing his dressing, I suspect, and left the tablets unguarded on his bedside table. The consultant's treatment proved dangerous though not in the way anyone imagined.

In a different situation, I would champion Dad. But in this case, it really doesn't seem worth it. Feeling disloyal, I reassure the sister that of course we won't pursue litigation. I will be able to talk him out of it, I say. 'No harm done,' I say, and ask for a wheelchair so that I can take him home.

As I push him finally off the ward, he resists all staff efforts to say goodbye and instead shakes his fist and bellows, 'you'll be hearing from my solicitor!' As a departure, I must admit it has pizzazz. Perhaps during that first and ridiculously long stay in hospital, this is what he should have done: threatened legal action. It certainly guarantees a quick exit.

Mid-June 2018. Vile brew

Dad is home for the time being but seems disorientated. Mr MS and I realise that we will have to start popping in to see him every day, at the very least.

Life becomes more pressured and the amount of attention some vegetables require begins to seem ludicrous. Take my overwintering onions. You'd think it would be enough to grow them all winter, then water, weed and sprinkle them with wood ash all spring. But no – they have specific harvesting requirements too. Once their green tops keel over in summer, you're meant to bend over any stragglers and leave them all in the soil for another fortnight. You must make sure to lift them on a sunny day, leave them on top of the soil a few more days then move them to a 'warm airy place' for a few weeks, covered with 'thin cotton' as protection. Finally, if you have any energy left, you plait them into a bunch.

That's more care and interest than I have going spare at the moment, so I wait until most of the onion tops are bent over then decide to just dig them all up one afternoon. It isn't exactly sunny, but it isn't raining either. Sadly though, onion after onion comes out of the ground no bigger than a shallot. I lean on my spade. What was the point? 50 tiny ones went into the ground last November and six months later, 40 only slightly larger ones come out. 'Big deal,' as Dad would say. I move on to my radishes. These are even worse. They have no bulbs at all; they look like dark pink question marks. They are so hard and fibrous that even Dad's super-sharp knife from the shed can't cut through them. What a wash-out!

To cheer myself up, I decide to revisit the auld family custom of home brewing and make my own fertilizer. Into a bucket go some nettles (I have plenty of those) followed by cold water. Then I go home, satisfied that at least I've done something useful.

I don't know if you've ever soaked nettles in a bucket? Floating around the plot in my floral gardening gloves and floppy hat the next day, humming as

I fill a basket with fragrant sweet peas, I have no idea of the disgusting stages of filth and putrefaction I am about to witness.

Over the next few weeks, as the nettles decay and the water turns black, it grows white blooms which become a feeding-ground, breeding-ground and general seething-ground for a thousand blue bottles. I have never smelt anything so foul. It's unfortunate that I've stood the bucket near the bench. Even that filth meister Mr MS is unable to drink his coffee in its vicinity. But we are both scared to move it.

When the three weeks have passed and it's early July, I plunge a Tupperware container into the vile brew, ready to dilute it ten parts to one in a watering can. I hold my breath but can't resist a little sniff to see if the smell is still that bad. It is. I nearly spew but press on and give the roots of everything on the plot a good dousing.

Afterwards I throw the decomposed gunk on the compost heap and give the bucket a thorough rinse. I can't help noticing that the flies have reassembled around the plants I've just fed. I give the plants a mercy drench with clean water and make a mental note not to use the Tupperware box for Mr MS's sandwiches. Not unless he really annoys me.

At home I wave my fingers under Mr MS's nose. 'And that's after five washes!' I say. He blanches. Is it admiration I see in his eyes? Or just wind from eating home grown cabbage? Either way, I decide I'll use shop bought fertilizer in future.

I have to admit that allotmenteering is hard work, perhaps too much right now, what with Dad. I resolve to give it a break for a couple of weeks and think about whether it's time to give it up. Not that I do think about that in my fortnight off. I'm too busy thinking about Dad and about why Mr MS is able to eat three times as much as me without putting on an ounce.

Walking to the allotment after the break, I steel myself for a bleak scene with weeds everywhere and wilting crops.

But the broccoli has shot up. The courgettes have produced five impossible yellow flowers, and the carrots have a strong if feathery presence. I also notice that my new comfrey patch is coming on. How wonderful it is to have an allotment, I think. How satisfying, how worth the effort! And doesn't Bob Flowerdew say that comfrey makes even better fertiliser than nettles? Apparently, it smells even worse, too. But just as it's impossible now to remember wanting to give up the plot, so it's impossible to remember bad smells. Into the bucket go handfuls of ice green velveteen leaves and furred blue flowers, followed by cold water. Then I get on with a few other jobs, humming as I fill my basket with fragrant sweet peas.

July 2018. Well-meaning professionals

Now that Dad is a regular at the hospital, his home becomes a Mecca for well-meaning health professionals. They treat it as an extension of their own workplace, leaving folders about and striding here and there with an annoying, proprietorial air. The week Dad turns 95, he receives two memorable visits, neither of which goes exactly to plan.

Concerned about his mental health these days, I've booked him another assessment and a young woman comes, another member of the flowery dress brigade.

'He's very deaf these days,' I tell her at the outset, noting her light, quiet voice. 'It's best to keep things short and loud. And practical.'

The possessor of a light, quiet voice myself, I know it's hard to change it just because someone asks you to. But the young woman does the opposite of what I'd requested. After a few brief questions about the alphabet, the date and the prime minister (even I can barely remember who that is, what with all the changes recently) she crouches down in front of Dad and in her light quiet voice embarking on a seamless, endless spiel about the benefits of mindfulness and meditation. She has obviously learnt it by rote. She seems unaware that he can't hear her.

'Look,' I interrupt. 'Dad's a man of his time. I don't really think...'

'Oh no, you'd be amazed,' she says. 'I have plenty of clients your father's age who find meditation really helps them. They enjoy recollecting happy memories.'

I picture them: polite elderly ladies happy to think about their grandchildren for ten minutes while whale music plays in the background. Don't get me wrong. As an anxiety-disordered meditator myself, I know the value of twenty minutes of calm. But I also know that meditation ain't Dad.

'But Dad's a man of action,' I say.

We both glance at him, marooned in his recliner with his heavily bandaged leg and dishevelled air.

'Well, he used to be,' I qualify.

Thinking perhaps that I am a mindfulness naysayer, she counters by turning to Dad again and embarking on the value of gratitude lists and counting the breaths. I go hot and cold, knowing that any minute Dad is going to react. I'm just not sure how. And then I find out. He slumps forward violently in his chair, head lolling and arm dangling over the side of his recliner.

She stops talking abruptly. She looks horrified. 'Ted! Are you okay?' she asks urgently, touching his arm. I feel sorry for her. 'I'm sure he's okay,' I say. Indeed, he 'comes round' immediately. 'I'm so sorry,' he says. 'I suddenly felt very faint.'

'I think we'd better leave it for today,' I say, standing up to usher her out into the hall.

'Of course,' she says. 'I'll just write up my notes.' She sits down next to Dad. Five minutes later, she's still writing.

'Can't you do that in the car?' I want to ask but can't, thanks to a lifetime of over-politeness. I do ask her to relocate onto a chair in the hall, however. While I make Dad a cup of tea, I hear her shuffling papers out there and wish she would just go. 'Go before Dad says something very rude about you,' I silently urge her. But at least, with Dad's deafness, he has no idea that she is still on the premises.

The second visit is from Occupational Health.

Still refusing to use a stick, Dad has become more adept than ever at 'furniture surfing.' It seems increasingly unsafe, so I'm delighted when he entertains the idea of a Zimmer frame, having used one in hospital.

But the OT who comes to assess him stares in horror at his floor, a flaky pastry of rugs and pieces of old carpet from the various homes that he and Mum lived in for 50 years, all laid on top of the existing fitted carpet. 'If you want the NHS to supply you with a Zimmer,' the OT tells him, 'you'll have to take up these rugs.' She points at a particularly big bump on the floor. 'I mean, look at that. It's a health hazard.'

Dad accepts this news in silence. But the next time I go round, he has been down on his hands and knees with a screwdriver. Everything that ever flapped, overlapped or curled at the edges is screwed down into the floorboards. In the kitchen, where there's a cement floor, he has glued the rugs to the lino. It must have half killed him. I am at once appalled and impressed.

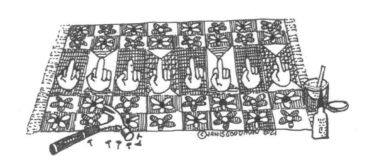

I ring the OT. 'Following your visit,' I say, 'Dad has secured all his rugs firmly to the floor. It's a lot safer now.'

'How do you mean, secured them?' she asks.

'With screws,' I say. 'And superglue.'

There is a short, frustrated silence. 'They'll all have to come up again, I'm afraid.'

'You're not prepared to come and take a look?' I ask. 'He's done a thorough job. Those rugs aren't going anywhere.'

'That's hardly the point,' she says.

We manage another couple of exchanges before I realise our conversation isn't going anywhere either, so I thank her and hang up. I've got an idea. Five minutes on Amazon reveals that Zimmer frames are as cheap as chips. I buy one and take it round to Dad's flat a few days later. I pretend it's the NHS one, of course.

August 2018. Currant affairs

Back at the plot, we face a late summer heat wave. It defeats many allotmenteers, especially those furthest from the taps. Broad beans go black and onions are overpowered by the soil turning to concrete around them.

Currants and berries, however, flourish to the point where harvesting and preparing them turns into a task in a fairy tale, set by a tyrannical king – impossible to complete within the span of one human lifetime, especially when added to the onslaught of plums that's just starting. I become enslaved to a group of fruit trees and soft fruit bushes.

This is by far the largest crop we have ever faced. I resort to deliberate mental strategies to enable me to tolerate sitting, night after night in the flickering blue light of the TV, plying my paring knife with fingers as stained as Lady Macbeth's.

First, I tell myself that the repetition involved in topping and tailing is like a meditation. Dad's mental health assessor would approve. But this delusion has a limited shelf life. Next, I try channelling my granddad on my mother's side. I never met him, but he was a market gardener as was his father before him. I'm getting in touch with my agrarian ancestors, I tell myself as repetitive strain injury kicks in and I have to down dose after dose of ibuprofen. It's in my blood. But once the novelty of this thought wears off, it's a quick plummet into good old-fashioned resentment and irritation. Why does no-one name and shame this aspect of allotmenteering for what it is: a pain in the arse? Could it be because most allotmenteers are men who have brainwashed their wives and children into setting to with their bowls and small knives without complaint?

But even as I formulate this nasty accusation, I know it's rubbish because most of the plot holders on our site are women. Perhaps they have very helpful partners, though in my experience the level of fanaticism required to sustain an allotment through all weathers tends to be an alienating factor in a relationship rather than a unifying one.

To be fair to Mr MS, he is outwardly helpful. But his preparation of plums, gooseberries and black, red and white currants is conducted at a pace so outstandingly slow that I suspect a form of passive aggression is at play. I am reduced to shouting 'get into the rhythm of the work!' a phrase once used to manipulate my own work rate as a fat teenager slapping joints of topside on the heat wrapping machine at Sainsbury's. It didn't work as a motivator then and I'm sure it won't now. I only escaped by showing an aptitude for the cigarette kiosk.

As for the raspberries, they don't taste so good after freezing so I decide we'd better eat as many as we can fresh. Here, Dad's short term memory loss comes in handy.

We sit in his living room while he munches from a full punnet. These days, it's not worth trying to talk while eating is underway. One thing at a time and all that.

'I shan't have any more,' he says, putting the half empty punnet down at arm's length on the windowsill. 'Or I shall be running for the toilet.'

'I know what you mean, Dad,' I say. He frowns. 'What?' We go to and fro with this a couple of times.

He only gets my meaning when I shout at the top of my lungs. 'I WAS JUST AGREEING WITH YOU.'

'Well, why didn't you say so?' he says. I try and start a conversation about next door's ivy-covered tree, which he enjoys looking at from his window. I point to a large bird sitting on a branch and wonder aloud what it is. But as he looks out of the window, the raspberries recapture his attention. I'm not surprised. They are far more interesting than anything I've got to say, or rather repeat several times at high volume.

'Ooh look, fresh fruit,' he says. 'Nothing to beat it.' He reaches the punnet down from the windowsill and tucks in.

In deference to Dad's bowels, I wonder if I should intervene. I decide not. He's enjoying himself too much. And anyway I've got three more punnets of that size in the fridge, and that's only today's crop. I need all the help I can get.

September 2018. A change of scene

In early autumn, Dad is hospitalised a further three times. In between, Mr MS and I keep an eye on him at his flat, as do the District Nurses. His pills are legion and their numbers are many.

To simplify things, the pharmacy begins to deliver them in a tablet dispenser labelled with different times and different days of the week. But Dad has begun to struggle with the concept of days and weeks. 'The weekend comes along and messes the whole system up!' he complains.

Wanting a reminder he can grasp, when the packs arrive, he pops all the tablets out of their blisters and lines them up on the kitchen counter or the table, or stows them in the pocket on his reclining chair. One day, finding some in the fridge, I begin to doubt the efficacy of his methodology and realise that Mr MS and I will have to pop in still more frequently to supervise. Dad is currently on four lots of tablets a day. As Mr MS and I are both still trying to hold down some kind of a job, we work out that we can realistically only visit twice a day (one each). So I install a key safe and hire a local care agency to do the 8am and 10pm visits.

Their first visit is at 10pm. It's dark and Dad's forgotten that they're coming so he's not best pleased. I get a phone call. 'He told me to eff off and threw the tablets at me!' says an upset sounding woman. 'I'm outside the flat now. I don't know what to do.'

I realise immediately that this is a different calibre of operation from that run by the District Nurses. They are all tough as owt and would never take this kind of nonsense from Dad. I apologize profusely and ask if she's willing to try again. 'His bark is worse than his bite,' I say, thinking of Dog MS, who makes a tremendous fuss about new things before settling down abruptly to accept them. Five minutes later the woman calls me again. 'He swallowed them down meek as a lamb. He even thanked me for coming!' Nevertheless, because he threw pills Dad has been marked down as 'volatile' on the file. Carers from now on must visit in pairs, which is (naturally) double the fee.

A couple of weeks later a District Nurse takes me on side and says that Dad needs more care. She cites the fact that he no longer gets dressed and has cut the bottom of his pyjama legs to ribbons. I tell her it's because he wants to make bandaging easier. Ever practical, I think, ever unconcerned with looks. But she sees it as a step down. She mentions a lack of hygiene. 'That's why his leg keeps getting re-infected. In a care home, they'll keep him clean.' She also says that Dad asked her to get a gun and shoot him. 'I told him we couldn't do that,' she says. 'I mean, it's not what the NHS is all about.'

That's one way of putting it, I suppose. Mr MS and I have a talk. The DN has good arguments. But knowing how much Dad, the world's most independent man, would hate a home, we decide to hold out a little longer. It is one of life's ironies that he finds himself in this position when Mum, who had always liked the idea of a care home ('some company at last') died suddenly, from a stroke.

Towards the end of September, a DN finds Dad up a step ladder in his bathroom wearing just his pyjama top. His electric drill is plugged in at the wall, ready to plunge into a sink full of water. She phones me immediately. 'He could have electrocuted himself!' Dad, furious at being prevented from carrying out his plan, argues that he was only having a wash. 'The plug wouldn't come out. I was drilling into it to release the airlock.' But the next day he falls asleep on his perching stool while frying bacon and eggs. This activates the fire alarm in the care home above and with him being so deaf, they can't raise him. The police are called and barge Dad's door down. He wakes just as they arrive. 'Oh, hello,' he says, 'what can I do for you?'

There is another phone call, this time from the Care Home Manager. 'I'm afraid we must insist that your father stop cooking his own food,' she says stiffly. This isn't her decision to make, of course. But we don't want Dad burning the care home down, however much he claims he's at the ideal age to commit a major crime, since life imprisonment wouldn't amount to much.

With a heavy heart, I begin the search for a suitable care home. The one above Dad's flat is fiendishly expensive and doesn't have the best reputation in the world, nor the best report from the Care Quality Commission, so it's not really an option. I wish Dad and I had discussed this when he was more lucid. But the window for two-way conversation, never wide open at the best of times, seems to have closed.

I find two cares homes I like, with no vacancies. Then the leg flares up again and we realise we'll have to take what we can get if we want to avoid another hospitalization. A home I thought rather shabby and smelly has two rooms free. The manager, a kindly yet straight talking woman, comes to see Dad. She catches him in a helpful mood. He signs a form agreeing to a fortnight of respite care, though I'm not sure he understands what it means.

Indeed, when the day comes to leave the flat, he point blank refuses. We argue for an hour, during which he accuses me of trying to drug him to get my hands on his money. I am upset. Mr MS sends me to the pharmacy to get Dad's tablets. 'We'll talk man to man. He'll come round, you'll see.'

Sometimes Mr MS amazes me. I return half an hour later to find Dad sitting with his jacket and cap on and Mr MS packing his pyjamas and sponge bag into his old leather grip.

At the home we go upstairs to the room I chose, which looks out to the other side of the valley. 'Do you like it, Dad?' I ask, ever hopeful. 'It's adequate,' he says, but the anger has left him.

Downstairs again we are served tea and cake. It is lemon drizzle, and tastes eye wateringly bitter as though the cook has tipped the whole bottle of lemon flavouring in by accident. Dad doesn't seem to notice, though. He turns towards me in the rather elegant sitting room. 'A change of scene,' he says, and smiles.

October 2018. Love among the lettuces part IV

We're advised not to visit Dad too much in his first couple of weeks at the Care Home, to let him settle in. It is difficult to comply. But then a development at the allotments provides a diversion.

A few years ago, you may remember that we left Harry ashen faced and coke addled following his gender reassignment. The Lady of Shallot was disembodied in the shed, dreaming of handsome Hobby-horse Person. Well, on an afternoon visit to the plot, I notice that Harry has given birth to a daughter. At least I assume that's what has happened, as a mini-Harry has appeared next to the big one on our neighbour's plot. But there is no sign of the father.

Delightful as it is to hear the patter of tiny scarecrow feet (or whatever passes for them) I'm not sure how the Lady will feel. The loss of her entire body back in the day seriously affected her own chances of getting pregnant.

Also, what son-of-a-broomstick fathered Harry's daughter? There are suspects. First on my list is Ranking Roy, with his Rasta hat and black plastic dreads. His relaxed demeanour is attractive, I admit. Second is Stan from South Park. Stan isn't exactly a looker, being wider than he is tall, but perhaps he laughed Harry into (raised) bed.

Before breaking the news to the Lady, I spend a few minutes at Harry's plot trying to figure things out. He looks dowdy today, in rubber gloves and a tired, tiered hippy skirt. Single parenthood must be taking its toll. Mini-Harry on the other hand looks smart in an orange pinafore dress, green bow tie and bright blue hat with sunflower. She stands next to an apple tree that bears small sweet apples much beloved by pigeons. It looks as if she is being pressed into labour while still only knee high to a grasshopper! I feel mildly scandalised but on the other hand, I'm sure Harry could use some help.

I wonder if Mini-Harry's outfit might point to the identity of her father. But orange, green and blue aren't Ranking Roy's style at all and I don't think South Park Stan would take any interest in dressing a child. It was probably Harry who chose the clothes, or let Mini-Harry pick them out herself. Reluctantly I decide that clothing may not be the most reliable determinant of paternity. But before I turn to leave, something strikes me anew about Mini-Harry's expression. That spooky cool, that smile that doesn't quite reach the eyes – where have I seen that before? The answer is suddenly obvious. In hobby-horse person, the Lady's longstanding crush.

Oh dear. I walk slowly back to our plot. The Lady may see this as a betrayal of some magnitude. I wish I could have prevented it, but how could I? No human gardener can prevent scarecrow shenanigans. In our presence they loiter and loaf, but when we go home at night, they are together in the dark for hours with just the moon for company. Nothing interrupts them bar floods, shed break-ins and visits from the lads who steal everyone's pears and plums.

I open the shed. Deciding that the lady has been kept in the dark for too long, I tell her everything: in fact, I carry her head to the front of the plot so that she can see for herself. I'm expecting tears, despair. But much to my amazement, the Lady's smile doesn't leave her face for a second, even when Mini-Harry is in plain view. In fact, her eyes may even take on a dreamy, maternal look.

As for Big Harry, she gazes on him in what could only be termed open admiration. I am surprised and not a little relieved. Perhaps she likes him even more, now that he's a father? Perhaps his brave decision to assume the role of single parent has won her approval? Her reaction is an admirable as it is unexpected. And, as I return her head to its shelf in the shed, I feel sure that we haven't heard the last of this tatterdemalion love affair.

Early November 2018. New lease of life

At the Care Home, cleanliness is achieved, albeit at the expense of liberty. Never again is Dad to see the inside of a hospital. This is a result, as is the fact that he's eating well and enjoying chats with some of the ladies at the dining table. When the fortnight is up, we ask if he can stay longer. Dad himself has no idea how long he has been there. 'When did I first start coming to these places?' he asks me. Sometimes he says, 'When am I going to get out of this shit hole? I've been banged up here for years, for a crime I can't remember committing.' But he enjoys the view from his room and the fact that the ensuite toilet is only a few steps away.

He is also delighted by the fact that when I visit, which is often, he can push his emergency call button and ask for a tray of tea and cake. The cakes are delicious. The lemon drizzle overload incident was obviously a one-off. What's more, 'it's all free!' Dad crows. Hardly, I think. The fees for the care home are astronomical and he gets no government subsidy. I don't tell him that.

Talking of astronomical, down at the plot I spend £75 for someone to reroof the leaky shed before winter comes. This is another thing that would scandalise Dad, partly because the entire shed only cost £99 in the first place and partly because he'd have loved to do the job himself. Right up until the day he left the flat, he was still finding tasks to do. He spent several weeks making a plywood mount to fix his phone to the sitting room radiator. As he refused to turn the radiator down – he paid a flat rate for his heating, so liked to have it on full blast, winter and summer alike – the phone became a hotline in every sense of the word.

We discover that there are no real opportunities to do tasks in care homes. There are only contrived ones. 'Would your father enjoy making a model Eiffel Tower out of drinking straws?' asks the activity lady. I wheel Dad quickly out of her vicinity before he can reply.

He goes on looking for genuine projects, asking repeatedly for his tools. In November Mr MS and I finally dare to head off on a five-night break. Before we go, we bring in a few tools, probably out of guilt. Mid-break we ring Dad from our hotel room. He says he's fine and things are going well. He sounds very chirpy. We're surprised and not entirely reassured.

On our return we're summoned to the care manager's office. 'While you were away, Dad flooded his own room and the room below,' she says, managing to combine sentimentality and frost in one sentence. 'I must ask that you no longer bring him ANY tools. Under ANY circumstances.'

Dad's version of the story is more detailed. 'The cistern of my toilet wasn't filling properly and the handyman here is a waste of space! All I did was take it apart to fix it.'

But we're forced to confiscate his tools, a betrayal that feels almost as bad as getting him admitted to the Home in the first place.

He isn't beaten though. In the coming weeks, he works out that he can turn his TV on and off from his bed by aiming the remote at the mirror. He filches various items of care home cutlery and twists and bends them until a spoon and fork work as two different kinds of screwdriver. Then he takes his wardrobe door off – 'it gets in the way. The room works better without it' – and removes the safety cables from all the windows – 'Let's get some air into this shit hole.'

'And that,' says the care home manager during another tete a tete in her office, 'could get us closed down. I'm sure you understand.'

I nod, pretending I do. Inwardly I stay on Dad's side. When the handyman puts the cables back on the windows and replaces the wardrobe door Dad takes it surprisingly well. But I'm irritated. The room, in my opinion, worked better without them.

Late November 2018. Winter of my content

The last weeks of November are quiet, with Dad seeming more settled. After sporadic autumn attendance at the plot, I start visiting more regularly. A funny time of year to do that, perhaps, but as noted before, I enjoy 'low season,' when growth, even of weeds, is slow and plants can't gang up on you to water or harvest them. And even though I call myself an extrovert, I love being there when no-one else is around. It is the opposite of being in the overheated care home, where proximity with other people and the scent of their bodily fluids is the name of the game.

I persuade Mr MS to take an hour off from work/having a cold/writing illegible lists in his diary or whatever it is he does these days and come and enjoy the peace and solitude with me. As others in long term relationships may confirm, being with one's partner can be almost as nice as being on one's own. 'Oh, and while we're down there, we might as well prune the apple trees,' I say, 'to give the visit a focus.'

Mr MS, a kindly man, agrees, having known from the get-go that I didn't just have his well-being at heart. In Nigel William's comedy novel, *The Wimbledon Poisoner*, the main character's wife tells him 'you block me!' That's a line often repeated in our house too. But at the same time, we're happy to spend an hour or two blocking each other outdoors.

I speed walk on the way there because Mr MS says he only has 90 minutes to spare and we've already wasted 20 of those in the garage locating the pruning saw, which he 'put somewhere safe.' He ambles behind. It's a dynamic so familiar we barely notice it.

But once we're down there snipping, good humour and enjoyment reign. Following in Dad's footsteps I have recently bought a home blood pressure monitor so I can tell Mr MS all about the results therefrom, a subject that as a hypochondriac I find fascinating. He parries by listing Yorkshire football grounds and the sorts of pies they serve. The low burble of our utterances bounces lightly off each other's eardrums, with neither of us straining unnecessarily to hear them.

For a novice pruner, Mr MS ends up doing an excellent job. He also finds the top set of a pair of false teeth. I plant out my garlic and some autumn-planting shallots called Giselle. Because Mr MS has his walking boots on, he is able to firm them in. 'I'm trampling Giselle!' he cries nonsensically. So intoxicated am I by the chemicals in the soil, I laugh immoderately.

After he's gone, I take a few pictures of our progress on my phone. But all you can see is bare trees and earth. I give up and sit on my home-made bench to drink my coffee.

And that's when the main event happens. With a sound like a gunshot, the bench seat splinters and I fall through it to land on the ground on my arse with both legs in the air. It's so sudden, I don't even yelp.

Questions hurtle through my mind. 1. Am I hurt? 2. Why have my coffee cup and flask remained undisturbed on the bench arm? 3. Will I still be able to play table tennis tomorrow as planned? 4. Does this prove that my joinery skills are indeed as limited as Dad suspected? 5. What's the point of a comedy accident if it goes completely unwitnessed?

I am suddenly furious with Mr MS for having gone home. He will be sympathetic later of course, but what's that worth, compared to the brownie points I could have scored from my ability to see the funny side of things in the face of minor injury and major indignity? As it is, I have to extricate myself from the bench's innards alone.

Before starting on the long hobble home, I take a few shots on my phone camera and realise that one good thing has come out of it. The demolished seat makes an excellent picture.

December 2018. A care home Christmas

The bench is mended by reinserting some screws, much to my relief. The wood has only splintered on the edge; nothing is irrevocably damaged. Back at the Care Home, Dad too turns his attention to mending, to getting the drawers in his bedside cabinet to run smoothly. I wish I could get him down to the plot to mend my bench but still, the drawer project keeps him going throughout December. We are invited to the Home for Christmas lunch, and I think how nice it will be not to have to cook.

On the day Dad declines the invitation to get dressed so we wheel him pyjama clad to the little dining room, where a tree is festooned in gold tinsel and tables are adorned with silver crackers and red serviettes. It all looks very festive.

There are only two other families in. 'It's a bloody crying shame,' says senior carer Diane, advancing on us with a bottle of red wine. Her paper hat is akimbo. The carers are waiting on table today, which strikes me as an indignity. 'Just a small one,' I say. 'Get away with you,' she says, winking and filling my glass to the very brim. She is obviously a woman after Dad's own heart. She brings Mr MS a Coke and Dad a glass of sherry.

Then she brings three plates full of turkey, ham, Yorkshire pudding, gravy, roast potatoes and mash. She winks at Dad. 'You like your Yorkshires, don't you Ted?' Indeed, Dad tucks in immediately. Mr MS and I wait for a minute or two for potential carrots, sprouts and peas then feeling silly, dig in also. 'Perhaps there aren't any vegetables,' I whisper. I try and see what the other families are eating but we are all at different stages of the meal.

I consider going out to the kitchen to ask, but it feels awkward and besides, Dad is halfway through his dinner now. We finish our meaty platefuls.

'Delicious!' says Dad, patting his stomach.

As dessert arrives, we turn our attention to the crackers. Dad dons his crown. Unfortunately, he gets a pair of nail clippers in his cracker and sets to work with them immediately. A crescent of finger nail pings into Mr MS's bowl of Christmas pudding. 'What do you get if you cross an elephant with a fish?' we ask Dad five times at high volume.

Meal despatched, we wheel Dad out of the dining room and a relative calls from another table, 'What DO you get if you cross and elephant with a fish?' We all laugh.

Back in the room we put the TV on ready for the Queen at 3pm. 'Mrs Queen,' says Dad, his old joke, and we all laugh again.

But during her speech, he begins fiddling with the drawers of his bedside cabinet again and continues throughout the Wallace and Gromit film that comes next. Dad's room is hot and small and rather pungent. All those things I can cope with but continuous drawer fiddling takes things to a new level of claustrophobia. Mr MS urges me to go out for a short walk. 'The cold will help you calm down a bit,' he says. It is certainly a relief to be outside in the chilly darkness but it's poignant gazing up other people's driveways into their uncurtained, jolly looking Christmas evenings.

On my way back to Dad's room I sanitise my hands at the dispenser in the hall and overhear a loud conversation in the sitting room between residents Keith and Bob.

'Do you want a banana?' asks Keith.

'I can't hear a word you're saying,' says Bob.

'Well, I'm seeing a doctor on Monday,' says Keith,' and getting my ears sorted. Nine o'clock sharp.'

Back in Dad's room, we sit with the TV and the drawer fiddling a while longer. Sandwiches and tea arrive and soon after that, there is a staff shift change. Mr MS drives home to have a chat with Dog MS and feed her. To my alarm he comes back with Dad's tools hidden inside a Christmas wine bag.

'What if someone sees?' I hiss.

'Don't worry. The night staff don't know about the tool ban.'

Dad, for his part, is absolutely delighted. With the correct tools, he's able to prise the defective runners off his bedside cabinet and install another set, prised from his other chest of drawers. The other chest of drawers is ruined but Dad couldn't be happier. He downs tools and grins. 'Thank God that job's done at last,' he says. I couldn't agree more.

January 2019. Sincere apologies

Attentive readers may remember that Dad is the sole tenant of our plot and that years back my plea to the Parish Council to register us as joint tenants fell on deaf ears.

In the New Year I decide it's time to have another go. Online, I search tenancy agreements from allotments nationwide, hoping to find an established protocol that I can bring to the Council's attention. I'm in luck. Allotment regulations all the way from Barnsley to Oxford allow allotmenteers to amend their contracts to include friends and family. I copy a few key clauses and boom, a carefully worded letter is on its way to our Council.

I don't have to wait long for a reply, although it isn't what I expect. The Council write with sincere apologies. They changed the rules five years ago, they say, and are therefore now happy to accept me as a joint tenant. I'm both relieved and annoyed. Why didn't they tell me? The letter and accompanying research have taken me several hours. It's impossible for a writer to just dash a letter off, don't you know: each word, comma and full stop has to be carefully chosen.

Also, while Dad would have relished this news as recently as a year ago, I don't think he'll understand it now. Fond of saying each January, 'Well, I made it through another Christmas. We've got the allotment for another year,' this year the milestone has gone unremarked. In fact, he doesn't appear to remember the allotment at all. He has literally lost the plot. Nevertheless, I decide to tell him.

I have taken to driving Cheeky Looks. I wasn't expecting to like it but I do. Thanks to Dad jacking the driver's seat up three inches with a block of wood, it's very comfortable for someone short-waisted like me who can barely see over the dashboard in a normal car. The sound system is beefed up by an extra speaker, wired in and attached to the steering column. The car has got a lot of poke for a tin can and like Dog MS, can turn on a sixpence. On the road outside

The Care Home, I wait a few minutes to let a Dyno Rod lorry out, then drive into the grounds and park easily in a little space into which a larger car would have struggled to fit.

On my way past the Manager's office, I'm beckoned in – and offered a seat. I anticipate trouble.

I'm not disappointed. 'Dad has been taking off his leg bandages and putting them down the toilet,' says the Manager. It's difficult for her to get the right tone for this announcement. The incident is no-one's fault. Still, she has had to pay for Dyno-Rod to come out and wants to blame someone.

'I'm most terribly sorry,' I say, 'I really am.' This is similar to the Council's apology to me i.e., not going to help much. If anything, the Manager's expression hardens.

Down the corridor, Dad's door is propped open, a good sign. He is sitting in his chair by the window, wearing the green and red felt elf hat he was given before Christmas, which he has taken a shine to.

As I go in, a carer pokes her head around the door. 'Who's a naughty little elf, then?' she chortles. Dad, more deaf since entering the care home, is unable to hear but recognises that some sort of joke is being made and gives a thumbs-up.

He smiles as I come in, another good sign. Sometimes these days he gazes at me dispassionately and seems to forget that I'm his daughter. He confuses me perhaps with Mum or with some other familiar-looking but ineffectual woman who has come into his room to badger him. It's as if the roles he has held throughout his life have begun to fall away. It isn't surprising, the way the Care Home infantilise their inmates. Or perhaps the regression is part of ageing and the Care Home is just responding. Either way, the mystery we sometimes sense at the heart of another human being seems deeper now in Dad, more impenetrable.

But today he looks pleased to see me. 'Hello Dad,' I beam, and bend over to kiss his cheek. 'Fancy a cup of tea?'

He can't hear, but quickly grasps a mime and says, 'that's a good idea, love.'

What a comfort a cup of tea is, and has been throughout my lifetime! The boiling of the kettle, the warming of the pot, the making of the tea, the waiting for it to cool, the drinking of it, even the washing up of the cups; all aspects provide a welcome ritual that takes the edge off life, much like the rolling and sealing of a pinch of tobacco in a cigarette paper. I think of the allotment, and my tea-making paraphernalia there that draws the process out even longer. I once stayed in a house in Italy with no running water, so the ritual included fetching a bucket of water from the well. Happy days!

Here at the care home, it merely involves leaving Dad with the paper I've bought then going into the kitchen and drawing hot water down from the vast steel urn onto two teabags in two mugs. But even these minimal actions are consoling. The chef, Alan, tells me that Dad has eaten cottage pie for lunch and had an ice cream and we agree, with much enthusiasm and certainly on both sides, that this is a Very Good Thing.

Back in the room, Dad turns the paper's pages in a slow rhythm. I place his tea for him and wait until he has drunk some of it before trying to speak again. 'Remember the allotment, Dad?'

He gazes at me, seemingly without comprehension. I write the words on a piece of paper and hand it to him. GOOD NEWS! THE COUNCIL HAVE GRANTED ME JOINT TENANCY OF OUR ALLOTMENT! But he glances at the note without appearing to read it and lays it to one side. His eyes drift back to his paper and he starts turning the pages again. Perhaps he is keeping my note to read later; perhaps not.

I smile. Like many other things involving Dad, I wish I'd tried to sort the tenancy out again a few years ago. But never mind. At least I'll be keeping the plot. For now.

February 2019. Veg shopping

Later winter is upon us, the start of a time known in the gardener's world as 'the hungry gap'. Cabbages, broccoli and stored potatoes are largely polished off, if not by humans, then by other creatures with various numbers of legs, or even no legs, or at least not legs as we know them. And nothing is yet ready to reap in the spring garden.

The hungry gap brings an annual difficulty. I need to go and buy vegetables in a shop. As mentioned in previous chapters, no self-respecting allotmenteer wants to do this. And now that my annoyance with the Council has worn off, my pride at being a bona fide plot tenant makes me realise that a self-respecting allotmenteer is what I have become, despite everything.

This is a wonder. But in the meantime, shopping must be countenanced if we want to eat stew, stews being my main attraction in Mr MS's eyes. A bleak future vegetably speaking will stretch ahead of us if I can't overcome my resistance.

In the local supermarket, I approach the carrots. They are ten times as orange and twenty times bigger than any carrots I have ever managed to grow and as clean and as pristine looking as babies. I swallow hard then transfer four of their damp cool forms to my basket. That wasn't too bad, I think. We haven't got the right soil for carrots, anyway. Mine always come out multi forked as well as small, a phenomenon caused I'm told by the clay soil.

Nearing the onions, my pulse quickens. My onions too always come out small, more like shallots. I string them up in the garage and say small onions are useful when you want to knock up a lunchtime soup for one, but it's hard not to feel shamed in the face of the supermarket's massive globes with their smooth, papery, pinky-brown skins.

I swallow my pride and tumble a few into my basket.

So far so good. A pack of Shiitake mushrooms catches my eye, and a whole coconut. I could never grow those, so perhaps I should buy some? But what sort of a meal could I make with them? I leave the question unanswered and go to stand in front of a display of dusty, dun forms piled up and fringed with fake parsley. This is a different order of difficulty. We grew a lot of delicious potatoes last year; all the varieties Dad likes plus some super knobbly Pink Fir Apple salad potatoes too, a pain in the arse to peel but tasting sensational.

The potatoes in front of me now are described merely as 'white.' They won't hold a candle to our home-grown ones. But as potatoes are a key ingredient of stew, I force myself to pick up a brown paper bag. I put my hand on a potato then at the last moment realise I can't do it. I turn away and pluck one of those pale green bombs arrested in mid-explosion – a cauliflower – from the shelf instead. There, that's something I have never tried to grow... yet.

I pay and exit, feeling both relieved and silly.

Luckily, I have backup. I can send Mr MS out later, since he will go to some lengths (like living with me) to get his hands on a good stew. I may have shouted at him in the kitchen last month for buying shop potatoes but now I'm grateful he's not troubled by ridiculous sensitivities. Or at least not the same ridiculous sensitivities as me.

I'm not looking forward to asking him, but that's one of the hallmarks of a long-term relationship. Most of the swords are double edged, and the humble pie is free.

August 2019. Sir Lazarus

We skip forward. At the care home for the past six months Dad has been having good days and bad days. But his trips to the sitting room on his Zimmer frame to gaze at the papers there become less frequent and when August arrives, he spends most of it in bed, complaining of stomach pains. He barely eats and begins to look very frail. When we visit the care home, he barely knows we're there. One awful day at his bedside, the doctor tells me he may not have long to live. A hospital bed arrives and he is put onto end-of-life care, with morphine every hour.

I cry in the care home manager's office. Back home, I cancel normal life for the foreseeable future and am in thrall to vivid childhood memories. I contact relatives and old friends. The Home advises me to appoint a funeral director, and I do. Their presentation pack includes two packets of Forget-me-not seeds. A nice gesture, I think, though Dad would prefer King Edward potatoes as a memorial.

Mr MS is a rock. For a fortnight, our sleep is conditional: every night we expect to be woken in the early hours by a phone call.

We're surprised then on our next visit to the care home. Alan the chef accosts us in the corridor, beaming from ear to ear. A shock, as we've got used the staff respectfully casting their eyes down when they see us.

'He's just eaten fish and chips for lunch!' says Alan.

'What?' I stare, wondering if Alan is confusing Dad with someone else. But he can't be. It's a small care home, and Alan knows everyone.

'You mean he's out of bed?' I manage.

'Oh yes,' says Alan. 'He's had some apple crumble too. With ice cream.'

209

We hurry down the corridor to Dad's room. We find him sitting contentedly in his chair, picking his teeth with a splinter from a wooden stirrer. 'Ah, nice to see you,' he says.

I'm too shocked for niceties. 'You're out of bed,' I shout.

For once he hears me first time. He shrugs, finding my accusation unremarkable.

'But you were so poorly,' I say, unable to catch up with events. 'You've been in bed for weeks.' This idea I have to repeat several times, during which he gets extremely bored by my attempt at conversation.

'I don't believe so,' he says. 'Now, I've just seen Alan go past. I expect you could do with a nice cup of tea.'

I learn later that the man in the room opposite Dad died in the night, totally out of the blue. It is as if, when the Grim Reaper came for Dad, he turned left instead of right in the corridor.

The following day, Dad reportedly eats eight Weetabix for breakfast. He also makes it to the sitting room on his walking frame to read the paper, after a month of almost complete immobility.

I take the Forget-me-not seeds to the allotment. Everything seems unreal. I don't know whether I'm allowed to feel relieved or not. I understand for the first time the expression *I don't know whether I'm coming or going*.

I wander around the plot until I find a shady spot. I read the instructions on the packet. It is too early to sow the seeds, in more ways than one, so I open the padlock on the shed. The combination is the number of my paternal Grandad's house in the 1960s, a number I chose because neither Dad nor I were likely to forget it.

Inside, I prop the seeds on one of the two triangular shelves Dad made out of plywood to fit the back corners of the shed. The Lady of Shallot's head grins from the other. The seeds will stay there until the time comes. I make a mental note to buy some King Edwards seed potatoes as well.

September 2019. Love among the lettuces part V

Talking of the Lady of Shallot, you may have been wondering how things stand these days between her and Harry. Well, in recent years they have been pretty low key, with the Lady's head perched chastely inside our shed and Harry consumed by the task of bringing up his daughter several plots away.

But visiting the plot in early autumn I realise that something wonderful has happened. They have run away together. This is particularly heartening for coming completely out of the blue.

To backtrack a little, the Lady seemed to have accepted and even begun to enjoy life without a body, grinning from the corner shelf in her bijou nook by the river. Dad's creosote was looking tired so one day I took the liberty of painting over it and the shed became a purple bower. The shade was at once feminine and vaguely Royal – as befits a Lady. I also installed a new window and a pink clematis to trail up over the roof.

The Lady became even more shed-proud. Every time I opened the door, I fancied the interior looked more neat and orderly. In between my visits, the Lady, I imagine, watched the comings and goings of allotment life. These happened by night as well as by day – the allotments suffered a rash of break-ins, though our shed always escaped. The Lady watched, with a sense of Schadenfreude no doubt, other people's sheds being ransacked, their tools tossed about and their fruit stolen. It was better than a soap opera.

I reported any news about Harry, as of course the Lady couldn't see his plot directly from her window. 'Harry's daughter has vanished,' I said one day. 'He must have sent her off to boarding school. They start them so early these days!' I brought news of former suitors too. 'Ranking Roy's hair has come off and blown away. He's bald as a coot!' The Lady smirked, safe in the knowledge that her flowing black bin bag locks were no longer exposed to the elements.

I noticed one day that something distasteful happened to Hobby Horse Person's eyes. Perhaps they were pecked out by a bird? Or perhaps they had washed off in the rain. One way or another there were now no eyes for his smile to reach, even if it wanted to. I spared the Lady that news, though I did tell her that his good looks were fading with age.

She seemed happy to be living life at one remove.

That's why I am so surprised to arrive at the plot this morning and find her shed door open, the padlock burst off its fixing. A further mystery: with no arms, nor even a body, the Lady surely didn't have that much bower-busting strength? I suspect Harry immediately. I glance across to where he normally stands. He is gone. It is as I thought.

I notice now that shed doors on other plots are open too. Allotmenteers stand around scratching their heads. And yes, it is a puzzle. Why didn't Harry go straight to the Lady's shed instead of going on the rampage? It seems he wasn't confident which shed she lived in. But then, I suppose it had been two years since he last saw her, long enough to lose her address. I'd have thought the purple paint was a dead giveaway but perhaps scarecrows are colour blind.

The Farmer seems very upset by the couple's getaway. He shouts, 'if I could lay my hands on those bloody buggers, I'd...' I blanch and turn away.

213

I check the inside of the Lady's bower. Nothing seems to be missing. Other plot holders say that some of their tools have been taken, but minutes later they find them scattered on the ground. The pair must have thought the tools would come in handy but then decided against it. I conclude they've opted to travel light.

The line 'everybody should run away once in their lifetime' comes to mind from an old film. I have never run away myself but I can't help taking my hat off to those who have. I imagine them living out their days in bliss together in a farmer's field somewhere in deepest darkest North Yorkshire. Good luck to them, I say.

Early October 2019. Last legs

A month after the scarecrow lovers' cheering escape comes the day I've been dreading. Dad is taken ill with stomach pains again. He stops eating and less understandably stops speaking, communicating only via sign language. No-one knows why, though in the past few weeks he has become so deaf that he now can't hear his own voice. 'Can you hear me?' he has kept asking, refusing to believe us when we've said yes.

Entering his room one mellow morning, I find him looking especially frail. He gazes across at me, impassive, and I'm reminded of primitive man peering out of a cave. When I do the cup of tea mime, however, he gives me a weak thumbs up. Re-entering his room with the tea I'm amazed to see that he has swung his legs out over the side of the bed. I put my arm round him and support him as he sips. He drinks the whole cup.

Despite this minor miracle, I'm called into the manager's office on my way out and told that Dad probably doesn't have much time left in this world. Days rather than weeks, she says. I've been told this before, of course, but how many miraculous recoveries can one man make? I shed many tears and over the next few days, Mr MS and I visit frequently. Dad is now on a special mattress that inflates and deflates automatically, to avoid pressure sores. It lets out sudden hisses that make us jump. Dad, back in bed now, seems unaware of it, and of us.

Dad moves slowly and inexorably towards his end. We've witnessed this process in other residents, passing open bedroom doors to see them bed-bound, impossibly skeletal yet breathing on. It makes you wonder how much a human being can be reduced and yet still live.

One night we are sitting with Dad when he suddenly sits up in bed. When I move towards him in concern, he takes both my hands and looks me right in the eye. Then he falls back, his attention going inwards again.

Returning, I think, to the pressing matter of dying. I get the feeling he has just said goodbye.

We go home, and sleep little. Dad survives the night but the following morning looks even more frail, if such a thing were possible. I sit next to him and hold his hand and it seems to me that his breaths are growing farther and farther apart, like midnight waves in a lazy summer sea. And then it happens. He gives a surprised gasp. And then is still. Despite knowing it was coming, it is a tremendous shock. I burst into tears. 'He's gone,' I tell the carers hovering at the door. 'I think he's actually gone.'

Kerfuffle follows as the carers elbow me aside to check his pulse (or lack of it) and open the window, apparently to let his spirit out. I don't remind them that this is Dad we're dealing with, so his spirit will depart in its own good time and not necessarily through the window, thank you very much. Instead, I think of all the things he loved – dogs, trees, Django Reinhardt, a good Rioja – and wonder where those enthusiasms have gone now he is no longer around to feel them.

I call Mr MS. When he arrives, the carers advise us that we may need counselling. There will be no shame in it they say, not even for Mr MS. It is kindly meant so we take it on the chin. Then they leave us in peace to wait for the doctor.

This is a blessing. We are able to sit with Dad in the hot, fetid little room that has become, as Bones used to say to Captain Kirk, 'life Jim, but not as we know it.' We gaze out across the courtyard at houses Dad latterly insisted were the ones he'd looked out on as a young man working for the Post Office in Dursley, Gloucestershire. The bed goes on huffing and puffing in an unsettling manner.

In the care home kitchen, Mr MS makes us a cup of tea. When he brings it in, I well up. 'How sad that it's only two cups, not three.' 'I could make him a cup too,' says Mr MS.

We decide not, but note that sitting quietly drinking tea in Dad's room is so similar to our recent routine, it's as though he's still alive. 'Should I do the Codeword?' I ask. It was another ritual. I'd buy Dad the paper, pass it over and he'd pull out the puzzle supplement and give it back to me. I'd act delighted. Except it wasn't really an act.

I decide against the Codeword. Instead, I hold Dad's hand (still warm). One death reminds us of others. Mr MS and I talk about his parents' deaths, then my Mum's. When Mum and Dad first moved up North, Dad became enchanted/irritated with the local greeting, 'Y'alright luv?' When Mum was lying in her hospital bed in a coma, he tried to bring her round by saying it loudly several times in a cod Yorkshire accent. We didn't know whether to laugh or cry.

No greeting is going to bring Dad round now, though. In a way it's just as well. He'd had enough of life, or rather life as an infirm old man, a state he found outrageous right to the end. He seemed to think he should have been made exempt. Perhaps he should have been. We clock up a good couple of hours before the doctor arrives to certify the death. Those hours mean everything.

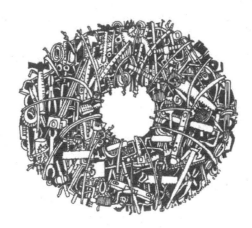

In the following days, there is plenty to do. Dad's opinions pop into my head, in his exact voice. My first letter of condolence comes from local government. Although they quote his National Insurance number and first name correctly, they get his surname completely wrong and refer to him as Mrs. In my head, he is incredulous. 'Who are these idiots? Can't they get anything right?'

Every day he has something to say. 'Look at that mountain of flesh!' he exclaims when I see someone overweight. When someone makes a silly mistake, he says, 'he hasn't got much between the ears.' 'Screaming brats,' he says, when children pipe up in coffee shops.

I don't know what to do with his voice. I assume it's just a phase. But my normal, mild-mannered self is terrified that one day his words are going to pop out of my mouth. But if they do, I hope people will forgive me. I am my father's daughter, after all.

November 2019. RIP Dad

Dad's voice is present to me throughout his funeral. It's a tiny affair. But the important people come. My two cousins and their wives drive a long way to get to the little chapel at the undertakers, halfway between our house and the allotment, as do some very dear family friends. I think how pleased Dad would be to see them. Two care home staff and four close friends of Mr MS's and mine come too ('What are that lot doing here?' comments Dad. 'Come for the free booze no doubt.') We hold the funeral tea at our house, where Dog MS joins us.

Talk turns to the celebrant. We all agree she did a great job and some of us were struck by her warmth and experience. My female friends query, however, her slit skirt, bare legs and ankle chain, especially in winter. 'She must be having an affair with the funeral director,' says one. To be honest, I hadn't noticed what she was wearing, worrying throughout the funeral about whether I'd ordered enough vegetarian sandwiches. But now I say that if Dad had been present in a less inert form, he would have called her a brassy blonde. The term has sprung so quickly to mind that I wonder if it's now actually my term, not his.

In our right minds, my friends and I would try not to talk about another woman in such terms. But now we laugh our heads off.

Speaking of Dad's inert form, during the service I was relieved that the coffin was closed. I'd had Dad embalmed, thinking my cousins might want to see him before the funeral. I'm glad they didn't. When I visited him at the undertaker's, his face, covered in a creepy white lace veil, looked so ancient and mummified that I hardly recognised it. Other dead relatives I'd seen in the past had looked plumped up, better than they had for years. But I had to spend my ten minutes in the Chapel of Rest focussing on his hands, hands that had done so much over his long lifetime, brown and freckled and still very much Dad.

219

Home in a state of shock, I asked Mr MS if he'd go and take a look. 'Of course,' he said. 'I mean, I'm used to dead bodies from when I worked as a healthcare assistant in London.'

He came back green about the gills. 'I see what you mean. I think I offended the funeral director. I blurted out that I'd never seen anyone looking so dead. I mean, they've made him look like Ray Reardon.'

There is a weekend between Dad's funeral and his cremation. Even though it's cold and wet and there's nothing much to do on the allotment I spend most of it there clearing brown stuff, wet and dry, from the ground, and tidying inside the purple shed. It's full of memories. A stubby yellow pencil, sharpened with a knife, lodged in a specially drilled hole in a shelf. A rake made by hammering 4"nails into a piece of wood and attaching it to a broom stick with little wooden struts. A white tub of something brown and sticky saved from c 1979. A fork and trowel set so cheap as to be unusable. Assorted screws and nails stored in the bottom half of a cut off Tesco's orange juice bottle. On Sunday afternoon, I close the door on these mementoes, but only temporarily. I know they will continue to bring Dad back to me more than anything else.

The cremation is private, attended only by Mr MS and me. I have made a new dress to wear and manage to focus less on the catering arrangements and more on Dad, though I am slightly worried about the music I've chosen, which contains the lyric 'you fucked it, friend.' The funeral director, smart in his reassuring uniform of death and weddings, draws my attention to it beforehand. 'You do realise that the music you've chosen contains, err, profanities?'

220

'Yes,' I say. 'Does that matter? Is it going to offend anyone?'

He holds up his hand to reassure me. 'It won't offend me. I just wanted to make sure you knew.'

'Well of course I know!' I nearly snap. 'Do you take me for a complete idiot?'

Then I realise it's Dad talking again, not me. 'It's fine,' I say.

But while Mr MS and I are sitting in the crematorium chapel with the coffin, waiting for it to disappear on its runners behind the red velvet curtain (it never does: when asked later the funeral director says that isn't how things are done in Yorkshire) I find myself waiting tensely for the offending lyric and worrying that I'm committing a breach of public decency. There's always some daft detail lying in wait to take one's attention away from the matter in hand, it seems.

I think again of the celebrant's bare legs, slit skirt and ankle chain, another distraction, and draw comfort from them. We are living in the twenty first century now, I tell myself. Perhaps these days, anything goes and perhaps, sometimes, that's a good thing.

December 2019. A natural memorial

In early December, we attend the Christmas party at the Care Home. I sit on the floor while the raffle prizes are awarded and carer Diane, who I have come to love and will miss terribly, tops my glass up continually with red wine. It is strange to be there without Dad, of course. It is also profoundly relaxing.

The next day, I turn to the task of his memorial, something we never sorted out while he was alive. It wasn't because we didn't try. One day, over coffee in his flat and well before his health declined, he said, 'when they ring you up and tell you the old man is gone, don't cry. I'll be alright.' This made me cry instantly of course, but he ignored my tears, turning his attention to an unusually detailed unwrapping of his Jacobs Orange Club biscuit.

'You're not frightened of death then, Dad?' I managed. 'Not at all,' he said. It was a good thing to hear. A little later I asked, 'and when the time comes, would you like to be buried with Mum?'

Mum's ashes are in a family grave in Gloucester that also contains her parents, brother and sister. Dad shrugged. 'Not especially.' Perhaps he found it inappropriate to barge in on a family grave that wasn't quite his. He didn't know or had forgotten where his own family of origin was buried.

'How about a headstone in the cemetery here?' I asked. He frowned. 'What if it gets defaced?' 'Hmm. A commemorative bench?' There are many of these in our small town. But the one near Dad's flat is favoured by youths. 'I'm not paying for a bunch of yobbos to sit about drinking lager,' he said. When I relayed this to Mr MS later, he was surprised. 'I don't know why. I think it would be quite fitting.'

We shelved the question for the time being. Of course, it ended up getting shelved permanently and now suddenly Dad is dead and there's no plan. But at least I know he had no strong wishes. I talk to my cousins and we decide to take Dad's ashes to Cheltenham, where Dad was born and lived as a young man. We commission a plaque commemorating his Mum, Dad and brother too and get it installed at a natural memorial site with views.

Then Covid 19 arrives and our plan to meet and scatter the ashes in spring 2020 is indefinitely postponed. But before that, I have an idea. Six memorial trees stand on one side of our local cemetery, separated from our allotment only by the local sewage works and ten thousand rabbits. I ring the Council to ask if there is room for a seventh. I'm prepared to be told there isn't or that they don't approve my choice of tree, an aspen that will one day reach an enormous height and dwarf the six ornamental rowans and cherries. Even if they do agree I'm expecting it to be expensive, going by the eye watering cost of buying even a tiny plot to bury ashes. But I'm put straight through to a lovely gardener who lets me talk about Dad then says that if I buy the aspen, he'll help me plant it. He will let me put up a memorial plaque, too. 'They're not allowed, strictly speaking. But we tend to turn a blind eye.'

'That's fantastic,' I say. 'How much will it cost?'

'Oh, it's free of charge, love. We think of it as beautifying a public space.' This is like being in the 1970's again, I think, but in a good way, when organisations didn't try to extract money from you left right and centre. I thank him profusely. I may be slightly teary.

The aspen sapling proves difficult to find. I visit the wintry back fields of several garden centres, poking around in sodden grass to try and identify leafless trees with no labels. There seems nothing online either. Then I remember a tree nursery an hour away where, during my stint of attending courses, I learnt how to graft an apple tree. I ring. They have aspens.

Mr MS and I go to pick one up. The tree is a beauty but 3' taller than they said on the phone. Mr MS and a bearded lad wrestle it this way and that but it won't fit in the camper van. 'Sorry about that,' says the lad. 'We'll have to deliver. £45 to your area.' I wince and they try once again, unsuccessfully. 'Never mind,' I say. 'At least we've seen the tree. At least I can pay for it now.' But their card machine isn't working, so I'm advised to pay on delivery. However, when the tree is delivered a week later, the driver has no way to take payment. 'It's best if you ring 'em up, love. Put it on the plastic.'

223

Before doing that, I arm myself with the tree and a four-foot stake and meet the gardener at the cemetery. As suspected, he's my age (about 21) and wears similar shabby gardening garb. We could be twins. We pick a good spot for the tree. I feel like a lightweight watching him dig into the hard winter ground but he says it's good exercise now that he no longer has to dig graves by hand.

We talk trees. He tells me the region's rarest and most majestic trees are located in a park about ten miles away. We both know this park as a no-go zone, with drug dealing at all hours. I wonder if I have the balls to go. I imagine standing with a friend in our gardening hats, peering at leaves and bark and making notes while groups of hooded youths exchange small packages.

Job done, the gardener and I shake hands. Once again, I thank him profusely, and may be slightly teary. I install my plaque, which is plastic but nevertheless looks jolly good. 'Not many walk by this spot,' he says as a parting shot. 'But some do. And one or two will notice that a new tree's gone in, and appreciate it.'

Back home, I ring the nursery to pay for the tree. 'Hello love,' says the man at the other end. 'Yes, I remember. The aspen. I'm sure you've paid for that.'

'I'm sure I haven't,' I say. 'I remember you paying,' he says.

'Perhaps you remember me trying to pay. Your card machine was broken.' 'Tell you what love, I'll check the books when I've a minute. If you owe me, I'll call you back. How does that sound?'

'That sounds good,' I say.

Of course, the call never comes. And if there was ever anything guaranteed to please Dad more than getting a beautiful tree planted in his name a stone's throw from the allotment and for nothing, I'd like to know what it is.

About the author

Mandy Sutter grew up in Nigeria and Bromley but now lives in Ilkley with her partner and a large dog. *Ted the Shed* is her third full length book. Scarred and inspired by her experiences on the plot, nowadays she restricts her gardening activities to the small vegetable patch and greenhouse in her front garden, a stone's throw from the A65. To find out more, visit www.mandysutter.com

Also by Mandy Sutter

Permission to Stare, Slow Dancer Press, 1994
Game, Smith¦Doorstop Books, 1995
Are You She (with Sidura Ludwig, Polly Wright & Myra Connell), ed. Lesley Glaister, Tindal Street Press, 2004
Travelling with the Bedouin Women of Hawd (with Amina Souleiman), MAMA, 2007
The Asylum Seeker (with Amina Souleiman), MAMA, 2007
Stretching It, Indigo Dreams Publishing, 2013
Old Blue Car, Kettlebell Press, 2015
Bushmeat (winner of the *New Welsh Writing* awards 2016), New Welsh Rarebyte, 2017 and Parthian Books, 2024

About the illustrator

Janis Goodman has worked as a cartoonist and animator and now focuses on illustrations and etching. She regularly wins awards for her work. In the last few years she has won two Printfest Awards and one at the Wildlife Art Exhibition, Mall Gallery, London.